DOMESTIC VIOLENCE

PROFITEER$

One Mother's Experience with

Police, CPS, DA and Family Court

A. M. CAZARES

Contents

PREFACE

While budgets are finite, justice is being denied to domestic violence victims, because police refuse to report and the DA's office refuses to issue a protection order, and Blue Privilege is the unwritten policy that provides impunity for abusers.

Government offices and programs designed for victims of domestic violence exists, but agencies seem to never have any funds to offer any meaningful assistance to victims.

It is my experience that in 2020, the American government continues to accommodate and provide preferential treatment to abusers, typically male, while dismissing the victim's experience--often denying protection, services, and ultimately, justice.

I decided to write this book so that sharing my story I might help other women struggling to understand how to get out of a seemingly hopeless situation. You see, I was that woman. I was living with an abusive spouse. I wanted to leave but was so beaten down, it was difficult just to perform the basic duties as a mother. Where would I find the strength to gather up my children and all our belongings and move across the country? Just getting through the next 24 hours was a feat. When my abuser decided he was "done" with me, I was sideswiped with a tsunami of hatred and aggression that would flood over me and my children.

The same man who took me before God, his family, and friends was now my predator who would not retreat. His volcanic rage was unpredictable as it was unrelenting once it started. I never met a person who could scream, yell, and rage for HOURS.

In different forms, he would project all his hatred and anger on to us. It was something I had never experienced. Unrelenting harassment, humiliation, and degradation. It was frightening and overwhelming. My children and I were deeply affected by the unrelenting verbal, emotional, and psychological abuse we experienced on regularly.

This book covers from the time I escape a brutal marriage that was spiraling dangerously out of control to the present. A journey for freedom, peace, and justice. It has been 10 years since I had a gun put to my head that August night in Arlington, Virginia. I was told I would die that night.

Isolated from my family and friends for the first time, I was lost and virtually alone in Washington DC, trapped with my abuser.

In telling my journey for hope and freedom, I want to inform women, especially mothers, what to expect when you leave an abusive relationship. Do not believe all the ads and literature. Sure, there are programs, offices, staff, and salaries, but rarely is there any meaningful assistance for women fleeing violence.

There are several reasons why I wrote this book but to do so now, in August of 2020, is to honor and celebrate the centennial of American White women gaining the right to vote. On August 18, 1920, the 19th

Amendment was ratified. It would be another 45 years before Black women would gain the right to vote through the Voting Rights Act of 1965.

The suffragists of the 19th century had few role models on how to be political activists in an undeniably male-dominated world. It was a brutal, hard-fought battle that fierce American women did not back away from. They held steadfast to the bold concept and determination that women had the same rights and privileges as their American male counterparts. Namely, the right to vote.

On this 100th anniversary of the 19th Amendment's ratification, let us remember the extraordinary courage and determination suffragists embodied to bring about revolutionary change for all American women.

Anna Marie Cazares

Deep in the Heart of Texas

August 26, 2020

A. M. CAZARES

DISCLAIMER

Some names and identifying details have been changed to protect the privacy of individuals. This book is not intended as a substitute for the legal advice of lawyers.

DEDICATION

This book is dedicated

to every human

trapped and oppressed

by domestic violence.

May humanity unite

to free you

from abuse and violence.

A. M. CAZARES

INTRODUCTION

Lessons from the Fourth Grade

I was fortunate to attend school in southern California in the 1970s. Our school rooms displayed the ideals and speeches of Dr. Martin Luther King, Jr., and President John F. Kennedy. We said the pledge of allegiance every morning and were allowed 'a moment of silence'. The teachers and curriculum were amazing. Every teacher I had during those years was passionate about educating us for the future.

Every teacher during those incredibly impressionable years were committed educators. Spelling lists were given every week throughout my elementary school years. Every day our teachers had a lesson plan that kept the classroom an active, living, breathing, learning lab for our young minds. Our school was less than an hour from the heart of Los Angeles. Field trips to the La Brea Tar Pits, Museum of Natural History, and local venues were normal and expected. It was an extraordinary learning experience that heavily influenced how I would parent my children. Keeping each day an exciting adventure of exploration while reading books and learning to count.

By the fourth grade, we began each morning with a routine task of "current events." We all were required to copy what was written on the chalkboard. It was an exercise initially to encourage us to practice our printing. A few words were always underlined in the current event paragraph. Our teacher would take the time to discuss the news event, reviewing the highlighted words, and try to explain what was happening in the world.

We learned about Watergate in the 70s to the kidnapping of Americans in Iran in the 80s, and all the significant events in between. The year I graduated, 1981, I graduated midterm because I had satisfied all my credits--and I wanted out. I wanted to get on with my life. I thought I would always remember this moment in time. How understated that single thought was.

On January 20, 1981, I watched President Regan's inauguration as well as the release of our 52 American hostages that had been held in Iran since November 1979. I knew that moment was history in the making. Thank you to all the teachers who made learning about the world interesting, understandable, and accessible. Most of all, you treated us with respect. My teachers explained very complicated matters to young children, so we could better understand and think about our world. When I look back on those days, it is hard to believe how much we expected to learn and master. Yet we always rose to the expectation and spelling always mattered.

Another important lesson that would leave a life-long impression was the idea of critical thinking. It appeared in many assignments. Whether it was language arts or math, it always came with a message of "critical thinking". We always had to be thinking critically. Questioning and assessing the situation, and always thinking about possible solutions. As a child in the fourth grade, I did not understand why the school psychologist would visit our classroom weekly. She would conduct psychological exercises on us as a classroom and later with a small group of advanced students.

The exercises would describe a situation, a hypothetical crisis, and the students were asked to think about: What 10 items would you bring to the deserted island after being shipwrecked? Or, which three people would you bring with you down into the underground bunker because there was a nuclear explosion above ground and life as you knew it no longer existed.

Some students would immediately start brainstorming. I would be sitting in my chair quietly freaking. I was imagining all the death and destruction we have just hypothetically experienced. All I could think about was: Where were my parents and siblings in all of this? I was always a bit shaken after those group psych exercises. Those exercises were shocking to me at the time, but it would be lessons from the fourth grade that would become my default in life. From those terrifying psychological exercises, I was instilled with the belief that I should always be thinking critically, especially during a crisis.

In the fourth grade, I learned how to prioritize, remain calm during a crisis, and plan to survive.

Working for a Living

I believe a lot of women go through their day at work questioning if this was what they are supposed to really be doing. Asking themselves if they shouldn't be somewhere else? Wondering if there was something else better going on? And if so, why are we there? While we toil away at our mundane job, often we do not realize that we are building our life and ourselves. We are gaining experiences and skills, learning about people and the world. Building knowledge and skills that can be called upon later when needed, like a superpower.

Los Angeles was a hotbed of drug and gang activity during the 1980s. You know it is bad when you look to Sin City, Las Vegas, as a haven. I was 19-years old and living in Las Vegas, Nevada. Work was easy to find and soon I found myself managing a real estate office.

Later I would accept a position as a mortgage loan processor at a federal bank. What I learned from those two jobs helped me buy my first, and three subsequent homes. Learning the process of how a home is sold and the financing process provided me with invaluable knowledge about real estate. Just as important, it trained me to document my work and forced me to read long loan documents. Typing documents, letters, reports, and answering phones for many years as an administrative assistant in the Los Angeles area always seemed like a go-nowhere job to me.

At the time, I only had my high school diploma, but yearned for a career. I wanted to do something exciting and meaningful. Instead, I was typing the same sales report week after week, month after month, year after year. Just before the end of the millennium, my life would take a dramatic turn.

In August 1998, I met, and would marry, a post-doc researcher, Dr. Michael Wichael. He was European and completing a mandatory post-doc year abroad. He had a senior research position at a prestigious university.

The courtship was all very whirlwind. What girl doesn't love a love story? Within months he was prosing marriage. I immediately put the brakes on the conversation of marriage, explained I was not going anywhere; no need to rush.

Within a year of meeting, I became Mrs. Wichael, a stay at home wife and mother. I kept myself intellectually stimulated with the endless conversations with my new husband. I also kept intellectually busy editing nearly all his research papers for publication.

Michael was a dedicated scientist and prolific writer. I enjoyed learning to write at his PhD level. I learned to meticulously edit and revise scientific research. Skills and techniques that would serve me well decades later when I needed to file court documents to protect my child.

I was not sure if I should write a book. After all, who am I? Outside of Aeolian Elementary Book Fair, I have never written a book. Not any type of celebrity or selling a product. At 57 years old, I am a devoted mother of two beautiful and brilliant children. I fulfilled my deepest desires with each birth. Although I have worked in a business office setting since I was 16 years old, I would weave my life with a mixture of administrative work, marriage, children, and the pursuit of a Bachelor's degree.

My love for writing steams from those early years at school. I am proud to be a product of a truly "old school" education system. Our teachers shaped and filled us with endless amounts of information, lessons, rules, and expectations. No matter what our level of intelligence was, we all were expected to rise to the occasion, and we did.

Finding Me

It was only after my divorce was I able to attend to my own needs, desires, and wishes full-time that I immediately went back to university to complete my long-awaited goal of earning a bachelor's degree.

I physically escaped from my marriage in June 2010. I drove my two daughters and myself back to the Austin, Texas area. That drive back home, back to where I own a big beautiful home which fortunately had not sold. Driving home, seemed like I was shedding off years of bad memories. I arrived a few days later ready to begin a new life. My life. After getting my daughters enrolled in school, readjusting to the new normal, I eventually applied for Texas State University.

All those years of going to night classes and Saturday classes. If you chose well, it all follows you. I was accepted and began the fall semester of 2012. Yes, I returned to school as a non-traditional student at nearly 50. Was it easy? No. But did I get it done? Absolutely. Why did I do it? First, it was a personal goal. Second, I needed to go back to work and support my kids. Third, I still wanted a creative career.

In the spring of 2014, I received a Bachelor of Fine Arts degree. Going to college is not easy for anyone, but to go back to school when you have children to care for is extremely challenging. It is incredibly challenging, but not impossible. When I graduated that spring, my two daughters sat proudly at one special ceremony.

It was from the Non-Traditional Student Organization (NTSO). Prior to the graduation ceremony, the NTSO club held a special event. I attended with my two daughters. We expected dinner and a speech. Instead what we were treated to, along with the other invitees and their families, was a lovely catered dinner and special ceremony acknowledging overcoming life circumstances.

Everyone knows how difficult college can be for any student, but to meet those demands while taking care of a family, well that is simply amazing. I have a wireframe mannequin which I hang some of my favorite necklaces and accessories. Among these, I draped my graduation cord across the neck and draped down the front, as it would be worn at the ceremony.

This is to remind me no matter what I put on; I always have that special recognition that I wear every day. Receiving a college degree was always a life-long goal. What I did not expect was receiving the elusive confidence I always sought—it arrived almost like a graduation gift to myself. What I also could not imagine was how integral that design education would be in gaining freedom and justice for my daughters and myself.

Speaking My Truth

The reason I wrote this book was to provide victims of domestic violence a true account of what it is like to exhaust every possible government which includes the police, family court, and social services and their respective programs. This book is giving an honest and accurate account of one mother's experience trying to receive help from the domestic violence I wanted to escape.

If you needed or wondered what it would be like if you left. Left the abusive relationship you find yourself trapped in. Millions of women, the majority being mothers with children, are trapped and opposed in relationships. Millions of victims are represented outside that family picture. Millions of gay and lesbian are affected by the epidemic of domestic violence that many do not seek help for fear of being doubly rejected.

Although this book will address the primary victims, the most vulnerable, mothers with children. For the ease of writing this book and for the reader, I will refer to 'women' or 'mother and child(ren)' with the clear acknowledgment that a significant amount of victims of domestic violence come from the gay/lesbian community and the sad fact that men are victims too.

What most people who have not experienced domestic violence do not realize is that when you finally decide to leave or call 911, you have been so abused that when the police, CPS, DA's office, social services, or the court system disrespects or dismisses you, it feels like being re-victimized. The feeling of being invalidated is exactly what goes on in domestic violence. The abuser is constantly enforcing rules and exacting punishment to those who do not conform.

Americans like to pride themselves on being the capital of freedom. If the measure of a nation is how it treats its most vulnerable, how does America measure up when millions of women and children are trapped in violent and dysfunctional relationships because of the police, CPS, social service, and family court?

The experiences I encounter are with a mother who truly was seeking help. I was not going out with the intent of surveying the effectiveness of our system. The system that our government spends billions on allegedly providing services for victims of domestic violence.

I am writing this book as an American taxpayer who is failing to see any good come from the tens of thousands of dollars I spend in my own community of Central Texas. I am failing to see in the state of Virginia a horrific pattern of abuse and neglect within its own system that is supposed to respond to citizens calling 911. Instead, the experience with local police just 30 miles from the White House. One might as well be calling the police in some third world country where women are treated, at best, as second-class citizens, and at its worst, women have no freedom or rights.

I am writing this book to help American women and children escape the unacceptable level of domestic violence we have come too comfortable with. I am writing this book to prepare women for lies on the other side of the front door. I am offering a sobering look at what our tax dollars provide: not much. As citizens of this powerful country, we need to do better. We need to do much, much better for the women and children of this country, for they are our future.

Women bring life into the world. We need to treat mothers with much more dignity and respect than we currently do. I do believe we treat children with the dignity and respect they deserve. In this socially connected, 24-hr news, and amped-up marketing and advertising consumer culture, I am afraid we are trampling on some of the most vulnerable in our society: mothers with children

I hope this book can serve as a learning tool for students and those working in social services, public health, government administration, etc. whose work it is to help and support victims of domestic violence. I also hope any person who is in the possible to affect policy on any level, let this be a tool for change. More must be done. More can be done. We must commit to making a drastic change in how victims of domestic violence are seen and treated as a victim of relentless abuse in their own homes.

Every day in America, millions of mothers and her children are not safe in their homes. They suffer domestic violence daily because they are forced to live with their abuser.

Companion Website

In speaking my truth, I have created a companion website to support this book. You can visit the website at:

www.amc-dvp.com

There I will display documents, communications, photos, audio, and other relevant information that tells my story as a survivor of unrelenting domestic violence in all of its ugly shades.

The website will chronicle my journey as an advocate for women and children still trapped and oppressed by domestic violence. I hope you will join me on this journey to make victims' lives more peaceful and safer.

CHAPTER ONE

How Did I Get Here?

SERENDIPITY, noun
Occurring or discovered by chance
in a happy or beneficial way.

MERRIAM-WEBSTER

California Dreaming

Growing up in southern California during the 70s and 80s was ideal. I was from a middle-class, Catholic family living in the suburbs of Los Angeles. The messages of influence I would receive growing up would come from my family, friends, school, and tv. That was it. That was all parents had to contend with.

The influence and messages from my culture would leave a lasting impression on who I would become. The message shaped my idea of who I wanted to be. It shaped my opinion of what others thought I should be. As I came into adulthood during the 80s, the message for young women was to maintain beauty and fitness while preparing for a demanding yet fulfilling career. In addition, women were to maintain their beauty, fitness, and allure while fulfilling their other roles of wife and mother.

Women in the 21st century enjoy, and take for granted, the hard-earned victories of the women's movement century earlier. Along with becoming a permanent fixture in the workplace, most notably, women gained the right to vote.

Americans in 2020 take it for granted that all Americans, men, and women, can vote. It was just less than 100 years ago that women gained the right to vote. With that right, the ability to cast a vote which has a direct effect on one's personal property, business, and inheritance. Having the right to vote meant having the right to influence lawmakers, speak about important matters of the day, and improve living conditions for the industrial workers. We need to ask ourselves: What are women of the 21st century doing with that powerful right to vote? What are we doing with the power to influence our lives and our society?

As a child of the 70s, I grew up watching my mother go off to work. It began as a part-time position as a maid, then full-time. After years of high quality and reliable work, my mother was promoted to the assistant housekeeper. Years later, she would become Executive Housekeeper for the Holiday Inn in Montebello, California. Even as a child, I understood and appreciated what an amazing accomplishment that was for a Hispanic woman with an 8th-grade education and five kids at home. It could not have been possible during the 70s without the unwavering support of my lovingly, devoted father.

My father, Ismael Ramírez Cazares, was born in Piedras Negras, Mexico, a border town with Texas. When his mother passed away, his aunts stepped up and made sure he was loved, well taken care of, and received a fine education. My father attended university in Mexico and received a degree in Pharmacology. By the time I was born in 1963, my father had already moved to the United States, served in the US Army, and had been honorably discharged. With my father's knowledge as a pharmacist, he served as a medic during the Korean war. Once he left the military, he would meet my mother while working in Los Angeles at a dinnerware factory. It was Los Angeles, 1958.

I always loved hearing my mom tell the story of how she met my dad. She was a single mother with two young sons. My grandmother had encouraged my mother to leave her brutally abusive, alcoholic husband behind in Mexico and flee to the United States. To make her escape possible, my grandmother convinced my mother to leave her sons, Armando, and Daniel, behind in Mexico. Once my mother had established herself, found work, and saved enough money, my brothers would rejoin my young mother in Los Angeles. This was an extraordinary plan for two Catholic women during the 50s. Back in those days, Catholic women did not divorce their husbands, no matter how abusive.

My brothers were very safe with my maternal grandmother, Emilia. She had a wild, independent streak that took her from Mexico to the California Central Valley and over to Colorado and back again. She owned a gun and knew how to use it. She also like to shoot tequila and knew how to shoot that too.

She would travel with her only child, my mother. They were inseparable and when my mother was a grown woman with a family of her own, that incredibly tight mother-daughter relationship. Even as a child growing up, I could see my struggle to be viewed as an independent entity, separate from my grandmother's control. While my brothers stayed behind in Mexico, my mother made her way up to Los Angeles, confident her sons were safest with her mother; no harm would come to those boys while they were in my grandmother's care.

My mother followed the plan and arrived in Los Angeles and quickly found work and a small apartment. While working at the large Los Angeles porcelain factory, she met my father. He was her supervisor, very handsome, and very single.

My mother possesses my grandmother's practical nature and assessed the situation realistically. She was an uneducated woman, on the run from her abusive husband, and two sons back in Mexico. My mother understood my father to be a college graduate, US citizen via his military service, single and no kids. With her prior experience with marriage, my mother was clear that she wanted nothing to do with her handsome supervisor. She did not need any type of man troubles. She was singularly focused on saving her money to bring her sons with her to Los Angeles.

For months, my father tried and get the beautiful and petite Maria Marketa Gomez to engage with him. Between my mother's natural shyness and her realistic grasp on the situation, my father's pursuit would not be easy. Luckily for me, both my parents were persistent in their goals.

My mother would explain to us how she rode the bus to and from work every day. While she was waiting for the bus to arrive, my father would pull up in his own nice, big car (in those days, a sure sign of personal and financial stability). My father would ask my mother if he could drive her home, and according to the story, she turned him down many, many times.

To me, rain has a magical quality it adds to the day. It tends to change everything: how the day looks, plans may need to be altered, and sometimes the day simply becomes serendipitous.

My mother waited at the bus stop as usual after a long, hard day of packing porcelain. She was soaking wet and exhausted. It had been raining heavily that late afternoon in Los Angeles when my father tried once again to engage with the beautiful Maria. This time the heavy rain would be just variable my father needed for success. That rainy day, the beautiful Maria accepted my father's offer to drive her home on that rainy day.

That reluctant ride home on a rainy Los Angeles afternoon would lead to a loving, committed, and respectful marriage that would span over half a century. I love the fact that my parents' first date was at a co-worker's wedding because their love story comes with a photograph. The company wedding was a big social event and my father was thrilled to take my mother as his guest.

I cherish that photo from my parents' first official date night. Neither of them knew that night that they would fall in love, go on to raise five children, and live every day of the rest of their lives, quite happily, together.

Giving Birth to Society

One of the most important roles a woman will perform in her lifetime is to give birth. In bringing life into the world, societies are built. Society is built from the labor women. Women who bear children are critically vital for our society, and for our species to continue. When women give birth, they are building a family, a neighborhood or community, a city, a state, and a country.

Yet with all this incredible ability and responsibility, it is my position that American women and their children are left incredibly vulnerable. "An alarming number of women in the United States experience grievous violence, and our government has failed to respond effectively to this crisis. Domestic violence is a human rights violation. While domestic violence is often treated as a private matter, the human rights framework provides a tool to challenge this perception and reframe it as a collective problem that society must address."[1]

The World Health Organization states that abuse becomes violence when it causes you to fear for your life. Violence impacts every part of us—physical, emotional, spiritual, and mental. Violence can be used with the intent to injure another person or destroy property. Whereas, aggression is generally defined as angry or violent feelings or behavior. Emotional abuse coexists with other forms of abuse and is the most difficult to identify.[2]

Non-physical acts can be violent. Domestic violence can occur between a parent and child, siblings, or even roommates. Intimate Partner

---

[1] Rey, Paola Garcia. *Inter-American Human Rights System Project.* Columbia Law School, Human Rights Institute, 14 Mar. 2011.

[2] "Violence against Women." *World Health Organization*, World Health Organization, 17 Aug. 2020, www.who.int/news-room/fact-sheets/detail/violence-against-women.

Violence (IPV) can only occur between romantic partners who may or may not be living together in the same household.[3]

The Centers for Disease Control describes the negative health outcomes due to IPV range from conditions affecting the heart, digestive, reproductive, muscle and bones, and nervous systems, many of which are chronic in nature. Survivors can experience mental health problems such as depression and post-traumatic stress disorder (PTSD).

The costs to society, a lifetime of economic costs associated with medical services for IPV-related injuries, lost productivity from paid work, criminal justice, and other costs, was $3.6 trillion dollars. The cost of IPV over a victim's lifetime was $103,767 for women and $23,414 for men.[4]

My Story is Not Special

The story of how I became a victim of domestic violence is not special. In the United States, over 43 million women and 38 million men experienced Psychological aggression by an intimate partner in their lifetimes.[5] American women and children live in domestic violence every

---

[3] Rutherford, Alison, et al. "Violence: a Glossary." Journal of Epidemiology and Community Health, BMJ Group, Aug. 2007, www.ncbi.nlm.nih.gov/pmc/articles/PMC2652990/.

[4] "Preventing Intimate Partner." Centers for Disease Control and Prevention, Centers for Disease Control and Prevention, 26 Feb. 2019, www.cdc.gov/violenceprevention/intimatepartnerviolence/fastfact.html.

day. My story is not special. I am one mother among millions in America who are forced to exist with domestic violence.

With all the programs available at the local, state, and federal levels, why are females experiencing more violence? In 2020, why are American women and children trapped and oppressed by domestic violence?

Violence against women has steadily increased over the decades despite spending over six billion dollars a year on programs for women trapped by domestic violence.[6] How can America be failing its most valuable citizens, mothers, and her children?

How is it possible to have millions of American women in need of shelter, counseling, and legal protection in America in 2020? Victims of domestic violence are trying to escape violence in their homes.

If you are lucky enough to have never experienced domestic violence, let me try to explain what it feels like.

It feels like living with a bully. Most people know what it was like to experience being bullied at some point in their childhood. It is awful, painful, and disturbing. Eventually, we learn to distance ourselves from the bothersome school mate or neighbor.

---

[5] Id.

[6] "Violence against Women." *World Health Organization*, World Health Organization, 17 Aug. 2020, www.who.int/news-room/fact-sheets/detail/violence-against-women.

Now imagine being a grown adult and the person you share a bed with evolves into a bully when it suits him. When he feels bad or is simply bored. When his ego is bruised. Frankly, there does not need to be a real reason, just the need to exert control and dominance over their partner. Abusers experience a thrill and deep satisfaction when they are abuse control, dominate, abuse, and threaten their victim.

Keep in mind that the is bully has access to you 24 hours a day, every day, much of it in person or on the phone. He can inflict his relentless emotional, physical, psychological, and sexual abuse whenever and wherever he chooses.

Taking the control and dominance a step further, the abuser will hoard the family money. The abuser will likely use the system (police, CPS, and family court) to inflict legal abuse. Dragging the victim through the system to rip the victim's child from her. This process often costs the parents thousands of dollars in court and legal fees.

The cost of a child custody court case can range anywhere from $3,000 to $40,000-plus. The huge range is due to the many factors that go into your overall court case and requirements for custody.[7] I was quoted from $4,000 to $20,000. That high bid also came with the disclaimer, "to start..."

You might wonder who would allow such a monster into their life? Let me try to explain who this covert operation works. First, the

---

[7] "How Much Does a Child Custody Court Case Cost?" Talking Parents, 31 Dec. 2019, talkingparents.com/blog/december-2019/child-custody-cost.

abuser/bully wins you over. Initially, it is fawning and flowers. All his attention is on you. He declares you are soulmates! He says you are his best friend. You are naturally flattered and let down your guard. The grooming has begun.

After the trap has been laid the victim willing accepts dates or a marriage proposal, the abuser will soon strap his victim into an invisible rollercoaster where only his abusive hand is always on the controller. Only he is aware of when you will be sent flying up or crashing down, slamming you sideways, or left locked in the dark. This unpredictable, inhumane, and destructive behavior leaves the victim frightened, anxious, and dysregulated. Disassociating from one's own body becomes the default for coping.

Over time, prolonged exposure to any type of abuse causes a more severe type of Post-Traumatic Stress Disorder (PTSD), a condition known as Complex Post-Traumatic Stress Disorder (CPTSD).

Why are American women and children running for their lives? Are we not the best country in the world? The most respectful to individuals and their rights? The freest?

We tout our American constitution and rights to anyone who will listen. What if America is not so great? What if the US government does not respect all Americans? What if some citizens are treated 'less than' by the US government? What if some citizens were denied their constitutionally protected rights? What if some American citizens are being systematically denied justice?

It is my opinion that the horrifying and repugnant truth is that domestic violence has become a profitable industry for the American Justice System and the legal industry that profits as well. While victims seek protection and services, US government entities (police, CPS, DA's office, and family court) receives US tax dollars, but systematically denies protection and services to American women and children, victims of domestic violence.

When I found myself calling a women's shelter in Falls Church, VA at 4 am in 2010, I had no idea that it would be the beginning of a 10-year odyssey for freedom and justice.

My story is not special. It is all too common. Way too common. So common, people overlook domestic violence acts as innocuous and fail to recognize that it is in fact, criminal behavior happening to us in our homes.

Experiencing domestic violence in your own home is such a frightening and complex experience. It is incredibly difficult to fully articulate the daily fear, threats of violence, and constant intimidation to not to tell anyone about the abuse.

Imagine being brutalized by the person you fell in love with, built a life with, had children with. It is unbelievably complex and emotional. We cannot just get up and leave. What the people do not understand is that victims have been conditioned to be fearful and compliant—all the time. Money is controlled by the abuser. We are trapped with our children. Where does a mother go with no money, food, or shelter? Victims are trapped in a violent relationship and in a home dominated and controlled by domestic violence.

Our Marriage was Killing Me

My story of domestic violence begins at the end of a marriage. My story is not special. The story of domestic violence is an ugly, brutal reality for millions of American women and their children. Living in constant fear leaves victims of domestic violence in a perpetual state of fear and anxiety. Depression is a natural and expected result.

Having escaped a brutal marriage, I can now tell you exactly why victims do not "just get up and leave". It is because we are trapped and oppressed by the multi-faceted aspects of domestic violence. It is not a one-time slap. It is often years of conditioning, degradation, humiliation, and threats. The threat to conform. The threat to agree to any demand. The threat to just comply with the abuser's requests--and nobody will get hurt, including her children.

The abuser does not have to physically crush his victim with his fists, he can easily crush her spirit and dignity with constant attacks. The abuser destroys his victim with hot, angry, profane, and vulgar words that degrade and humiliate her as a woman and mother. She is left shattered and traumatized.

When a battered woman speaks with the police, CPS, DA's office, or court staff paid to help victims of domestic violence, she is often disheveled, exhausted, exhibits poor concentration, struggles to speak and explain what has happened and what she needs. She may even present as mentally ill or homeless. It is this distraught appearance that unfairly justifies US government workers to treat victims of domestic violence with disdain and disregard.

What the civil servants fail to recognize is that they are dealing with a survivor of prolonged intimate partner abuse. Experiencing verbal abuse daily is degrading and destructive enough, but compound that with physical, psychological, and sexual abuse and what you end up with overtime is a shell of a person. What is left is the outer shell holding in all the pain, suffering, humiliation, and abuse privately. The shame is so great, the victim often suffers alone and in private.

When the pain becomes too much to bear, victims will end their own life. Tragically, the abuser will continue harassing his victim until a suicide or completely mental breakdown is achieved.

For me, it took years to begin functioning semi-normal. During the abuse, I would feel myself not being fully present. Afterward, I felt myself struggling to make simple decisions.

I did what no parent should be forced to do, I asked my eldest child to double-check my thinking. My child had lived in the house and knew what I had been through. My child looked at me with a tender mix of compassion and helplessness. She helped us survive those nine months we were forced to live the abuser.

He had cut off my access to money the day after his most brutal beating. My only goal was to get out alive with my children. I could not think of anything else beyond that. It was sheer survival mode.

This should not be happening to anyone. This should not be happening to American women and children, but it does. What I have been through is something no woman should experience. How is it that in one of the freest, richest, and most advanced societies in the world, millions of American women live in fear in their own homes? They exist on fear and anxiety with their children. They exist in a world controlled and dominated by domestic violence.

The reason I announced I was leaving my marriage was that weeks earlier, the specialist I was seeing for my unexplained pain and swelling, had informed me that I had Rheumatoid Arthritis. I sat there relieved, for just a moment. I was glad they knew what was wrong with me. I had been experiencing increasing pain throughout my body, I had gained a tremendous amount of weight and just felt like I was dying. I thought I might have cancer and as a mother, I did not, could not even say it out loud to anyone.

In silence and unwanted solitude, I thought about who would take care of my children. I pained at the thought of splitting my children. I had one child in each of my two marriages. They had grown up together. They would be losing their mother; they would be losing their only other sibling. I was devastated just thinking about the possibilities.

It would take months before results and a final diagnosis was given. When it was, I had a huge sigh of relief that it was not cancer. However, in the next moment, I was delivered the news that just overwhelmed me. My doctor informed me I had Rheumatoid Arthritis, and then she said the words that just leveled me: "It's a chronic illness. You will have to take medication for the rest of your life to manage it."

Fortunately, I had a phenomenal doctor. I trusted her assessment and outlook, yet I could help but feel this overwhelming sadness hit me. I asked the doctor how did I get this? Nobody in my family has this. Then it came. The answer to it all. Along with a few factors, she mentioned stress.

I knew I was living in a home and marriage with unmanageable stress. The daily verbal, mental, emotional, and psychological abuse had put my body through such a state of unrelenting stress, my body in flight or fight more, it had manifested into a chronic illness. My body was screaming, "Please take care of me!" and I did.

I immediately made plans to leave my marriage. Because of the constant and increased domestic abuse, it was hard for me to make decisions. I felt myself struggling to think, to process, and to decide. Yet I had to keep moving. As a mother, we do a thing for others that we would do for ourselves. Leaving my husband, marriage, and the life we plan was in the best interest of my children. Any ideas or fantasies of living happily ever after were incinerated. I need to make plans for a new, independent life.

After weeks of relishing the thought of freedom a new independent life, free from domestic abuse, I announced to my husband that I was leaving. I would move back to Texas with the two children (6 and 12 at the time) into a home I still owned, and thankfully had not sold. My husband acted unphased. He concurred with me and said he was "done" with me. Until the day I left, nearly a year later, he would repeatedly scream at me that he was "done" with me. I thought it was one more annoying habit I would not have to deal with in the future, but later I would understand he was announcing his elaborate plan for citizenship had come to fruition and he no longer needed me. He was done. No need for me anymore.

During the 9 months of being forced to stay with our abuser, one of his reoccurring rantings would be over his immigration. He would threaten me regularly, reminding me that if I "fucked with my citizenship" he would "put a cap in me". Yes, this Ph.D. and JD thought he was being a thug. I knew he would not risk everything, no matter how much he hated me. He is too self-serving to allow anything or anyone to interfere with him achieving his goal of becoming an American.

The Deadliest Time

With the women's shelter for battered women refusing to rescue me, I was left with few options. I tried not to panic, but if one is not panicking in a situation like this, when do you?

The thought of calling the police played out in my mind incessantly. In each scenario, it always ended the same: he kills all of us. I could not see a scenario where he would go down willingly. Where he would allow himself to surrender. He grew up in a country with a known Fascist dictator who was in charge for the first 15 years of his life. The dye was cast: He grew up learning you are either the oppressed, or you are the oppressor. He would never go down willingly. He would never admit defeat. If he was going, we were all going down with him.

My instincts told me if the police were to arrive at our rented townhouse in Arlington, Virginia, his new prestigious job would be toast, and all that we had worked toward would be gone. There would be nothing (professionally/financially) to live for. The abuser lacks compassion and I knew his thought pattern and chose not to take the risk. I made the difficult decision not to call the police that night because all the scenarios that played out in my head ended badly. Also, he was still very much in possession of the semiautomatic, as well as his full arsenal of at least a couple dozen firearms and plenty of ammunition.

I would carry the enormous guilt of not calling the police that night for years. Guilt for prolonging the horror of domestic violence on my children. I did not call that night and the next day while I assessed my black eye, bruised body, and pounding head, I wondered how in the hell did I get here? While I was trying to focus my blurred vision, I had to operate as a mother as though everything was fine. As though I was not living with a violent man who just tried to kill me last night. This is what domestic violence looks like and feels like. Trapped and oppressed by an abuser who enjoys dominating you through fear and violence. By threats and physical harm. By extinguishing any independent plans, you may have so you are existing only to serve them.

If the threat to the mother does not bring compliancy, the abuser will unemotionally drag the children into the negotiation. Immediately the mother folds, gives in to whatever degrading or humiliating act the abuse wishes to inflict, so long as he spares her child.

The child may escape direct abuse at that time, but the child does not escape the indirect abuse: witnessing its mother being abused. The child cannot help but absorb the daily degradation and invalidation verbal abuse causes. Over time, both mother and child are depressed from the relentless put-downs, insults, vulgar and profane language, unpredictable screaming sessions led to a breakdown of the person's spirit. What is left is a shell of a person, holding in all the pain and suffering, past and present, and operating on what is left of her Flight or Fight system.

Over time that physical exhaustion from being in a constant state of fear and anxiety, never knowing when "he'll blow up", manifests in the body. Headaches, stomach aches, and constant worry and stress will accumulate in the body. As Dr. Mate says, "The body keeps the score." When this type of high-level stress from living with an abusive partner accumulates, the victim often finds themselves suffering from a list of autoimmune diseases. I agree with Dr. Mate's theory that this is the body's way of saying no. No more will I allow you to subject to this incessant bullshit. Stop! Stop and start taking care of me, your body, yourself.

It would be several years later before I came across a report which stated exactly what I feared: the deadliest time for a victim of domestic violence is the moment she wants to leave.[8]

Although it took years before I allowed myself to be forgiven, that report validated my difficult decision, not to the police, and confirmed for me that my instincts had been right. I had made the right call that night. I was not being a coward. I was a mother thinking of what the best way was to survive an attack from within my home. I never slept again while he was home and awake. I slept on a separate floor. I would stay awake most of the night thinking of what my next move should be.

---

[8] Mitchell, Jerry. "Most Dangerous Time for Battered Women? When They Leave." Ledger, The Clarion-Ledger, 29 Jan. 2017, www. clarionledger.com/story/news/2017/01/28/most-dangerous-time-for-battered-women-is-when-they-leave-jerry-mitchell/ 96955552/.

Once he was off at work and my children were at school, I would collapse and get some sleep. I would wake in time to pick up my youngest from 1st grade. I needed to remain calm and as "normal" as possible. I need to keep us alive until we could get out safely.

What would he do if he heard or saw the police arrive? He would know instantly that his new, prestigious position in Washington, DC would be jeopardized? What I weighed in those early morning hours was: Would he kill me and our sleeping child or go with the police willingly? I had bruises and scratches all over my face and body. There was also a black eye and full fist print on my left (dominate) arm; there was no way the police would be able to overlook this obvious evidence of an assault.

I had never seen my husband that angry, that out of control. He certainly never showed his abusive side before we married. He was the picture of European refinement. When he asked me to marry him, I feared he would 'change' after marriage. He assured me he was the same guy all the time. Oh, how foolish and naive I was.

Weeks earlier I had announced that I was leaving the marriage. At the time he acted as though it was exactly what he wanted. He stated that the children and I could not leave the home fastest enough, because he wanted to get on with his new life. We had arrived in DC as a team and now that his first year as an associate was almost over, he did not need me around to spend his new salary. He said unemotionally that he did not love me anymore and that he was "done" with me. I was surprised. I expected a big fight, but he took it all rather calmly.

Abusers are like addicts in that they need a little bit more to get his abusive and domineering fix satisfied. Domestic violence escalates. The thrill and satisfaction the abuser receives from dominating and controlling another human being is a drug, a chemical drug in their brain that comes from the anguish created by the abuser. They feel powerful and in control. They are kind of their world, if only for some fleeting minutes. The abuse will return when the abuser feels weak and needs to remind himself and everyone around him that he is king, and no one is to question his wishes, rules, or expectations.

My announcement that I was leaving the marriage was an announcement that he was not good enough and that I was better than him. What I did not realize is that this announcement prompted my abuse to move into destroy mode. I was now the enemy that must be destroyed by any means necessary. He would carry out that mission for nearly a decade.

What I did not think about or expect was after that the brutal beating was the following morning our joint bank account and only credit card would be closed. My abuser cut off my access to any money. I would be forced to live with the man who had just beaten me with his bare hands and put a gun to my head for the next nine, hellish months. My children and I were prisoners in a home raging with domestic violence.

What I also had not anticipated was that this marriage would violently tumble down the moment my husband received his US citizenship that summer in 2010.

When I called the shelter that early morning in August of 2010, I began the long, arduous journey to seek help only to be denied and rejected for services by the police, CPS, DA's office, Legal Aid, and Family Court.

I was blessed to grow up in a family where I never saw my father disrespect my mother. He never raised his voice to her. Every day I saw love and respect between my parents. It was a wonderful way for a child to grow up, however, it left me ill-prepared for the real world outside my front door. I was completely unaware of the evil that exists in the world and that naïveté would make me an ideal target.

I grew up believing all those commercials and ads that if you were in a violent relationship there were organizations and services to help victims. The program messages tell you to leave a violent relationship. All you had to do was call and they would help you. They would protect you and keep you safe; all you must is just call them.

The shocking reality was that what I found with domestic violence programs and services offered by government entities is a façade. A false front with nothing behind it. Sure, there are lots of government departments, organizations, programs, and services created specifically to help victims of domestic violence. However, in my experience these special government programs are failing battered, American women and children.

They do little beyond setting an appointment, providing identifying information, and filling out paperwork, waiting around for a disinterested caseworker to speak with the victim briefly. The appointment is over, the information has been collected to justify they have "helped" a victim. The victim is sent home without resources, services, or counseling. Sent home to wait for the government's answer to the request for help.

Weeks or months go by before an answer is provided. In my experience, I was consistently denied any services. I found it interesting after the 7th or 8th time, that there was this reoccurring phrase they would say or write. You were rejected or denied help "due to budget constraints". It was always "budget constraints" that nobody in that government office could help a battered mother protect her children and herself.

The government employees certainly have money in the budget for their steady check, a buffet of benefits, paid holidays, train-cations, and retirement contributions, but there seems to consistently never any money left to help victims in any meaningful way. While the directors, administrators, caseworkers, and office staff collect a salary with a buffet of benefits, paid days off and mini-vacations disguised as training, I found no services, no shelter, no advocacy, no protection or services were made available to me as a victim of domestic violence. To add insult to injury, I was regularly treated with disdain, disregard, and disrespect at nearly every government office and appointment.

As a victim, I felt lost, abandon, and confused. I was being overwhelmed by my abuser and underwhelmed by my government. The good guys were bad, and the bad guy was worse than anyone could imagine. I felt like I was living some twisted tale where reality is really the unthinkable. I was a modern-day Alice in Wonderland, trapped on the other side of the looking glass.

It is in the government agency's self-preservation interest to keep victims in a constant state of need, so government bureaucrats can justify their requests for more money. No one wants to live with domestic violence, but getting out of an abusive home is impossible when you learn of the grossly unjust and incompetent behavior of government employees who are paid to help victims of domestic violence but undermine their freedom from violence and ability to seek and receive justice.

CHAPTER TWO

Arlington, Virginia 2010-2011

*The moral test of government is how that government treats
those who are in the dawn of life, the children;
those who are in the twilight of life, the elderly;
those who are in the shadows of life,
the sick, the needy and the handicapped.*

Hubert Humphrey
38th US Vice President
(1911-1978)

Falls Church Women's Shelter

It was around 4 am when my shaking hands reached for the big phone book. Thank goodness I did not toss it out. Instead, it sat there across from me in the basement of our rented Arlington, Virginia townhouse. The front of the book has a section of information pages and had exactly the information I was looking for: Domestic Violence.

There was a shelter nearby in Falls Church, Virginia, a city next to Arlington. For a moment, I allowed myself to imagine that my child and I could be whisked away that night. Safely rescued from an unfathomable scene of domestic violence. I was so shaken that I misdialed on the first attempt. I hung up, took a few deep breaths, and tried to calm myself enough to dial seven digits.

The call goes through and eventually was answered by a woman with a distinct accent. Filled with panic I described what I had just been through and begged for someone to come rescue us. Her first question was, "What did you do to make him so angry?" I was speechless for a moment as my trauma-filled brain tried to process this insulting question. I thought I had just dialed a women's shelter for battered women. Instead, I reached a ridiculously insensitive and ill-equipped person. I called for helped and found myself explaining what I did to deserve being beaten and my life threatened with a gun.

Our six-year-old daughter was asleep upstairs on the third floor of our four-story rental. At a moment when I did not think I could experience any more pain or disappointment, the woman on the other end of the telephone line said the most crushing news a victim of domestic violence involving a gun could hear, "We cannot come and help you. It is too dangerous for us. He has a gun." She then advised me to call the police and ended the call.

There I sat, battered, and bruised. My head hurt from the slugs he landed on my skull. I screamed for him to stop because he was going to kill me. He did stop. He got off me and left the bedroom. He headed up to the fourth floor. I laid there trying to catch my breath, control my sobbing, and assess what just happen and what I needed to do next. Before I could put any plan into action, my abuser re-entered the bedroom. He straddled me and put a black semi-automatic to my head and screamed, "Say goodbye to [our 6-year old child], because you're going to die tonight!"

The term "have your life flash before your eyes" is not fully understood until you are in the unfortunate position to experience just that. I had just been brutally beaten with a closed fist and now my abuser was on top of me and holding a semi-automatic pistol at my skull. He raged on spewing his hate for me. I had lived in Las Vegas for eight years and quickly assessed how bad my odds were. I honestly believed I was going to die that night. All I could think about is what would my daughter wake up to? Would he allow her to wake up at all?

In between these thoughts of motherhood which always foremost in my mind, were images of the most important times of my life. Images of my parents. Growing up in the endless summers of southern California. Childhood memories. The great loves of my life. Images of bringing both of my children into the world. These are the images that "flashed before my eyes" as though my brain knew it was about to be terminated and this was the last self-fulfilling act the self can do when faced with this situation, experience its life by remembering the most meaningful moments in one's life.

Fairfax County Court & Attorney Referrals

Over the 10 years since our escape, I have had to deal with the Fairfax County System. In both instances, they were grossly unjust.

The first encounter was after the August 2010 assault, I began calling some of the phone numbers listed in the phone book for assistance for victims of domestic violence. I called the courthouse asking for help. What I received was a referral to a few attorneys. I thought, "Great! These

are court-approved attorney to help women trapped in domestic violence."
I hoped they would be "low bono" which are significantly reduced fees.
"Pro bono" are unpaid community service hours attorneys are required to
perform to maintain good standing with the status of their professional
license. Either one would be great. I felt like I was gaining some traction.

I began making the calls, reaching out to female attorneys in the
northern Virginia area. One by one, I heard the same thing. There was
nothing free. Hours rates for consultation ran as high as $450/hr. This
certainly weeded out who could pay and who could not. Who could
receive fair representation or who would not? Who would receive help and
who would not? How is this fair to victims of domestic violence? How do
these attorneys get on this guaranteed gravy train of an endless supply of
true victims and the ability to coldly and calculating disregard those who
cannot afford the most basic representation in favor of helping only those
this the cash?

This referral service made by the court ensures more business for the
court. If you can pay, you do not get justice.

I would have to deal with the Fairfax County court system again in
2016 when my abuser would steamroll our divorce through a pal of his,
judge not-so-graceful. I contacted the court numerous times explaining I
was a victim of domestic violence. I explained my abuser was pushing
divorce papers through where I did not have an attorney and wanted those
papers pulled back.

Unfortunately, the person answering the judge's call was Barkwell,
Judge Judi Disgraceful's assistant. I did not know who Barkwell was but
apparently, Barkwell knew who I was. Strange? Not so much. You see my

abuser found a new girlfriend online and had moved her into the townhouse I escaped from less than 6 months earlier. This new girlfriend was a court worker and friends with Barkwell. So when I called BEGGING for help, asking specifically for any type of domestic violence program. Miss Barkwell said to me with all the condescension she could muster over the phone, "This divorce is going to happen whether you want to or not." I sat there speechless. What had I just walked into?

Legal Aid: Northern Virginia

During my 10-year odyssey to receive help and justice, I was referred to Legal Aid in both Texas and Virginia. I applied to both. I was told that I qualified for both. Yet both offices refused to help me. Yes, hard to believe, but this will be a reoccurring theme in the domestic violence business. All the professionals and administrative staff are receiving salaries, benefits, paid time off, bragging rights to their family and friends about how they are so generously devoting their lives to helping victims.

When in fact, they are receiving a paycheck to answer the call or hotline and eventually blow them off. They will initially listen and take your information, so they can add it to their stats that they interacted or provided some vague service. To justify their existence, they just answering the phone, telling victims how sorry they are, BUT they cannot help you in any fundamental way.

Funds just do not allow it. But here is a flier with the wheel of domestic violence that I know too well. First, by living it. Second, by being handed that same flier by everyone I encountered seeking help. It is you people who are receiving the salary, benefits, and retirement that need to study that damn flier.

Beyond the physical abuse, there are numerous ways to abuse a person. The psychological destruction of the person you live with. The emotional torment of a loved one whether is a partner or child. Verbal abuse is easy to administer any time of the day or night. Over time, it erodes and will eventually destroy the soul. From the daily insults to the endless criticism of everything you do to the all-out aggressive verbal assault where the abuser is following you around your home or has you literally corned in a room and the hot, heated, hate-filled words rage out of his mouth. Dispersed in between the insults, degradation, vulgarity, and profanity is the threat that you will never escape. You are their prey, and this is their game. They are in control and you must lose. Abuser climax at the thought of this level of control and dispense of abuse. In this perverted world, the highly dysfunctional abuser is finally king.

By the end of this book you will see how over and over, every agency, department, and office that I contacted to receive help or services, I was rejected, denied, and asked to leave. My ugly story of domestic violence was disturbing and effecting their NPR-listening, tea-sipping, office Zen.

CHAPTER THREE

Austin, Texas 2011-2016

In matters of truth and justice,
there is no difference between large and small problems,
for issues concerning the treatment of people
are all the same.

Albert Einstein
Physicist and Noble Prize Recipient
(1879-1955)

Legal Aid: Central Texas

As I explored the programs and services available in my local area of central Texas. Austin is the capital of Texas and has a bountiful assortment of social services. As I worked my way through the list of services and programs created for domestic violence victims, I was directed to attend a legal clinic where I could apply for free legal services.

The legal clinic was held one night in a school cafeteria. Dozens of volunteers and people in need of free legal help filled the tables in the room. I filled out the packet of forms I was handed. When a woman called my name and quickly scanned my paperwork. The details of my domestic violence caught her attention. She seemed to put a priority on the file and told me they would contact me in a few weeks.

Weeks would pass, then months. I would follow up with phone calls. Legal Aid was going through some type of phone system repair where the public was told to come into the office to receive a status update. I did this for over a year. Eventually, they said they lost the paperwork and I needed file again. I did that. Again, weeks and months would pass before I was told that I qualified for Legal Aid, but they just could not seem to find the funds to help me out in my case. I was out of luck once again.

Arlington, Virginia Police Department

After arriving back in the Austin, Texas area in June 2011, it took a while to get the children and me back to our new normal. We got out alive and now I needed to begin to rebuild our lives. One of my goals was to have our abuser held responsible. Once the kids were back in school schedules and hanging out with friends, I made a call to the place where it all happened. I called the Arlington Police Department.

A young male answered the phone. He announced he was a Public Information Officer. I explained had escaped a brutal marriage and was now safely in Texas. I asked the officer how could go about filing a report. He explained I had to come into their office to file the report. I restated that I was now living safely 1,500 miles away.

The officer was neither friendly, helpful, or compassionate. When I explained that I needed help filing a report because I had been brutalized in the Arlington area, the public information officer then informed me I was going to need a lawyer to file that report. The public information officer concluded the conversation with a remark that he was not giving any legal advice. It sure sounded like legal advice to me.

I have often wondered what *NOT* might have continued to happen to us. The domestic violence could have been knocked off its tracks if that "public information" officer had been the least bit compassionate and provided resources. How many years of domestic violence might we have escaped if that Arlington, Virginia PD employee had done his job fully, completely, and with an ounce of humanity?

Instead, I was treated like what I had been through was not the least bit important to the police. I was treated as though what I was asking for was too much. In my experience, the subject of domestic violence is incredibly common, yet the public servants being paid with public tax dollars behave as though it is a foreign topic.

Court and police staff act ignorant about the dangerous plight women are begging for help. The invalidation victims experience with a practice of "acting ignorant" about the topic. The employees will ask stupid, basic questions to have the victims exhaust themselves explaining what they and their children have been through, only to dump salt on the incredibly personal and painful disclosure with complete rejection.

I have been told by a Fairfax Women's program, "I don't know how to help you." Those words should never, ever be uttered by ANY person working in a domestic violence program.

Not only did I feel like I was in some type of messed up Twilight Zone episode, I felt like the Norwegian Expressionist artist, Edvard Munch, in his famous autobiographical painting, "The Scream". According to edvardmunch.org, the autobiographical and expressionistic image is based on "Munch's actual experience of a **scream** piercing through nature while on a walk, after his two companions, seen in the background, had left him."

Hopelessness: A Destination Nobody Books

I believe one of the most dangerous places for a victim to be, is in a place of utter hopelessness. No hope of getting out a sad, painful, unpredictable life of fear, anxiety, humiliation, and abuse. Victims may spend hours being brutalized by their abuser, but spends years trying to run or recovery from that traumatic, dehumanizing event that occurred most likely in the so-called safety of one's home and that hands of an intimate partner.

When the same person who you shared a deep, meaningful love life with becomes your abuser, it shatters the mind and soul. This deeply complex human experience is called cognitive dissonance in the world of psychology and counseling. For the human to try and hold those two immensely powerful concepts at one time is so disruptive to the human mind and spirit, it causes a profound disturbance, what professionals call Cognitive Dissonance.

The mind tries to reconcile both personality the abuser has presented. Mr. Charming and your abuser. The extreme concepts are so great, it causes trauma to the psyche. This trauma is visible on the victim. the high The answer is too horrendous to fully understand. The heart wants to exist safely in the good memories. The brain's self-preservation mode will not allow the victim to forget the horrific abuse that just occurred. The alarm bells to "get out!" are experienced by repetitive visual and emotional replays of the violent encounter. The brain is repeatedly sending the message this environment is unsafe. Get out! But you can't.

The abuser may have locked to the door to the house, room, or closet he put you in. He has likely moved you away from your family and friends or demanded you cut them off. He has isolated you. Now you have few resources to turn to. Not just for help, but even more important, to check your reality. This is how domestic violence brainwashing happens. Slowly, day by day, week by week, year by year. Until one day you wake up, battered, bruised, and realizing you are trapped in a home with your intimate partner and he has also become the greatest threat to your very existence.

Words fail to describe the devastating effects women face when their intimate partner and father of their child works vigorously to undermine the mother and his child's well-being, happiness, and success. The uphill battle women face every day is compound and made immeasurably more difficult when the primary male in the family is working against mother and child. This is the invisible cost of domestic violence that women and their children pay every day long after the separation has occurred.

National Suicide Prevention Lifeline

One of the few services that consistently delivered a compassionate presence over the phone (they also provide support by text), was the National Suicide Hotline. No one can prepare you for the depths of despair victims find themselves in while trapped in a relationship seeped in domestic violence.

Some nights were saturated in despair and utter hopelessness. I found myself sitting squarely where- no mother, no person, should ever find them: hopeless. When one is at the bottom of human existence, when looking up seems impossible, I am so grateful that our nation put funding behind:

National Suicide Prevention Lifeline

1-800-273-8255 (TALK).

Someone will be on the other end of the phone line 24 hours a day, 7 days a week. The **National Suicide Prevention Lifeline** is a United States-based suicide prevention network of over 160 crisis centers that provides 24/7 service via a toll-free hotline with the number .

It is available to anyone in suicidal crisis or emotional distress. The caller is routed to their nearest crisis center to receive immediate counseling and local mental health referrals. The lifeline supports people who call for themselves or someone they care about.

In July 2020, the FCC finalized an order to direct telecommunication carriers to implement **9-8-8** as the new toll-free nationwide telephone number for the hotline by July 16, 2022.

Please support this organization whenever you can. Consider donating during the holiday seasons when the need is exceptionally high for individuals in crisis or the depths of depression. If you or someone you know might need this resource, I encourage you to save it in your phone right now.

This organization performs thousands of lifesaving acts every single day. They saved my life.

CHAPTER FOUR

Man asses, Virginia 2017

There is one, and only one, thing in modern society more hideous than crime--namely, repressive justice.

Simone Weil
French philosopher and activist
Sister of mathematician, André Weil
(1909-1943)

Summer Visitation 2017

Six years have passed since our escape. Years of wrangling and delays finally provided me with a divorce decree that was finalized in March 2017. My children and I felt with the divorce finalized, we could finally get on with a normal life. All the fighting should be gone. No reason to fight. He got exactly what he wanted because he wrote the contract, denied me getting a lawyer, and filed it. Even when I protested at the court, I was ignored. Toyed with by the judge's clerks who are Molly Collie's BFFs.

We are supposed to be all adults here. For heaven's sake, were middle-aged! We are officially boomers, yet these grown women act like we are back in middle school with their petty, shallow, Mean Girl attitude. They were so incestuous in their relations; official court papers were handed to my abuser where he mailed them to me. Although it displayed the Fairfax Court address, it was hand-written, and postmarked from a US postal station near his home, not the one nearest the Fairfax County court complex.

This is their way of letting me know exactly how tight they were with the court personnel; and that he was totally in control of the process.

Call 911: Comedy Relief Arrives on the Scene

Just three months after the bitter divorce was finalized in March 2017, I believed the worse was behind us. Visitation was scheduled for 30 days over the summer break. We agreed to mid-July to mid-August. Although I went to great lengths to outline the conditions of the visit, namely have our abuser's arsenal of weaponry to be under lock and key throughout the 30-day visit.

Our child's plane scheduled to fly Austin to the DC area was not just delayed, it had been re-routed and arrived near midnight. The airline had not provided the box lunch they guaranteed for their unaccompanied child. Our child was 13 at the time and arrived exhausted, hungry, and unprepared what laid ahead.

For the next 30 days, day and night our abuser dished out daily verbal, emotional, and psychological abuse. Many people do not understand or care to believe the extent of what this type of domestic violence can do. It is not simply a matter of daddy who had a bad day and was being grumpy. I will describe what was told to me by the victim. The first weekend of 'summer vacation 2017' began with screaming sessions that took place while driving to and from getting pizza. The degradation and humiliation being assaulted upon our child were disturbing enough that Molly Collie who was driving, could not take it any longer and pulled the car over. The Collie got out of her car, found a bench, sat down, and began texting and calling friends.

Our child was left to endure the continued screaming match. It was our child's first visit since the divorce was finalized. We all believed the worst was behind us. That is when Molly Collie decided it was time to go home. Our child called me, frightened, upset, and feeling overwhelmed with the verbal assault that just occurred. She had just arrived a day or two earlier. What we did not understand, our abuser had a plan. A psychological plan to destroy our child's well-being. Even more sinister, there would be adults contributing to this abusive campaign. Grown women standing by encouraging the abuser or failing to call for help when things had obviously gone off the tracks.

It was a harrowing 30 days. Day and night our child would call me. Explaining that our abuser was grilling her. Questioning her about adult matters. Nothing had been planned, except for some wine festival. Our child was 13 at the time. The preplanned event and tickets purchased were for Molly Collie's enjoyment. As it turned out, when the weekend came for the wine festival, our child was feeling quite ill. Days earlier our child had complained about a sore throat and headache. On the day of the festival, the child had to persuade our abuser to allow her to stay home. The child did not feel good and saw no fun in going to a bluegrass, hot air balloon, wine festival for the weekend.

Our abuser escorted his honey to the festival while our child visiting her father for 30 days, stayed behind with a fever and headache. Over the next 48 hours, our abuser would relent and finally agreed to take our child to the doctors. Our child was immediately diagnosed with laryngitis and was given antibiotics.

Still, the abuse continued. The yelling and screaming. The degradation and humiliation. Day and night, I received calls from our child telling me exactly what he was doing and saying. I was horrified and emailed the description of his behavior.

The verbal, emotional, and psychological abuse reached a crescendo around midnight on August 7, 2017. Our abuser had been doing his non-physical style of domestic abuse. To follow a family member around the house, floor to floor, room to room all the while screaming obscenities and vulgarities no human should be exposed to. The verbal intimidation and degradation continue to all areas of the victim's life, loves, and interests. Item by item the abuser takes each cherishes aspect of the victim's life and puts it under scrutiny. Verbalizing and harshly criticizing the victim's life, loves, choices, body features, insecurities, accomplishments, goals, failures, and so on.

Our child "could not take it anymore" and called 911. What followed is partly what motivates me to write this book and consider a life working to change laws. No victim of domestic violence should ever have to experience what our child experienced when she called the police for help.

Nothing could have prepared us for the treatment our child received. In my possession is the 911 call our child made. It goes on for nearly 15 minutes. For 15 minutes, my child was begging for help. I can hear the panic in voice and her father raging in the background. Numerous times the Prince William County police dispatcher assures my child that help is on the way. All the while one can hear our abuser RAGING. He is unaware our child has called 911. Over those excruciating 15 minutes the call is dropped or hung up a few times to conceal the call being made.

Although I understand my child lived through the ordeal, any time I listen to the audio I find it gut-wrenching. It is amazing how brave my child was in the middle of one of the most frightening times of my child's life. I was nowhere present, and her greatest threat was coming from her father.

I challenge anyone reading this book, imagine being an adolescent and being in a threatening situation where you realize it is necessary to call the police for help. You are convinced immediate harm is just outside the door. Rage is being spewed and there seems no slowing down. This is what a child experiences in domestic violence. Unbelievable fear, anxiety off the charts, flight or fight defenses are on tilt. Yet we expect children to come through traumatizing events like this, perpetrated by a parent, or adult close to the child, and just get over it.

No adult would be treated this way if a domestic abuse call came into the police emergency line. However, my child was treated like a nuisance. Her fear and experienced were invalidated and dismissed. She was told, "This is your father's house and he can do whatever he wants." She was then directed to go to her bedroom. That is the most disgusting and vile thing I could imagine a domestic violence abuse victim being told. My child called the police for help, she received none. What she saw was

Officer Pfister yakking and laughing with our abuser. Yeah, apparently, it was Joke Time.

There is nothing funny about domestic violence. Prince Williams County's answer to domestic violence is to administer Comedy Relief to the abuser and ignore the victim. That is what the local police force of Manassas, Virginia did when a very brave girl called them for help. They accommodated our abuser with all the professional courtesy one can expect when both of you earn a living behind the Thin Blue Line.

The victim, a child, was dismissed and disregard. Although it was necessary for the Prince William County police officer to administer comic relief to the alleged perpetrator who appeared agitated, no report was taken.

Invalidating actions from so-called professional compounds and expands a victim's trauma. True fear and anxiety set in because you have just received proof that no one (who is supposed to help you) is willing to do so. Your pain, suffering, injuries, and trauma do not matter.

This is so abusive in itself; it has prompted me to share our story and this unfathomable behavior. Men who are supporting each other in secretly abusing their own family members. It is 2020. If the world knew exactly how unfree American women and children who are trapped in domestic violence. If American taxpayers knew how much money is set aside for domestic violence issues, but how little reach victims. Americans would be repulsed and outraged if they knew exactly how much was spent on overhead and how little if any, results are achieved.

One of the goals of this book is to raise awareness of every American adult. It is time to address domestic violence, in all its insidious forms. To continue to turn a blind eye to America's shameful secret is to be an accomplice to continued abuse.

CPS: We all Voted, and it is Not Abusive Enough

Reeling from the midnight rage episode, the next step was for our child and the abuser to meet a caseworker at the Northern Virginia Child Protective Services (CPS). Once again, the abuser was accommodating, and the victim was treated with suspicion. Our abuser is aware that we collect evidence whenever possible. The abuse is so pervasive, we all do our best to capture the insidious mental games our abuser taunts us with.

First, our child was transported to the CPS office by the abuser. Yes. As you can imagine the abuser used this time to interrogate and intimidate his victim, our child. Never taking any responsibility for the acute emergency, child barricaded in the bathroom for protection from raging father, a 911 call needed to be made. Help was needed by a child trapped by domestic violence.

After multiple calls to the social worker over a few days, I was stunned when she informed me that my child's situation was not abusive enough for them to investigate, to bother with. I had to ask, "How was this decision made?" She explained that in their morning meetings, they all discuss the cases and vote on which ones will be investigate and which will not. Our case was deemed not abusive enough. Services denied.

4 AM Letter to the Governor

After CPS'S preliminary interview, they took a vote like they do every morning. Unfortunately, my child's case received a thumbs down. Apparently, it was not abusive enough to "warrant an investigation". The abuser could take his laptop into the interview and play out of context material. My child was told by the caseworker, she insisted numerous times, "not to record the meeting."

Our child had recordings of the abuse she endures in the previous 30 days with her father, but the caseworker never asked the victim for any possible evidence.

I was furious when the CPS caseworker told me about their little daily vote. Every child's situation should be investigating, Hire more people! Put abusive people in jail! Do not just leave families, especially children exposed to abuse in their homes to continue to be subjected to domestic violence.

With nothing left to do I searched the internet for resources and ideas. At 4 am, I wrote an impassioned letter to the governor of Virginia. I explained the domestic violence we were experience and the failure of his Prince William County police as well as CPS.

I was surprised, the next morning, I received a call from CPS. Low and behold, my child's case had magically become important enough to warrant an investigation. The caseworker let me know that everyone on the floor knew about our case. The acknowledgment that one impassioned letter at 4 am can make an impact was enormous on a desperate parent looking for help.

A. M. CAZARES

CHAPTER FIVE

Austin, Texas 2017-2020

*It is a hallmark of the American system of justice
that anyone who appears as a litigant
in an American courtroom is
treated with dignity and respect.*

Maryanne Trump Barry
Retired Judge for US Court of Appeals, Third Circuit
Sister of 45th US President, Donald J. Trump

Travis County District Attorney: *Wildly Unjust*

Dealing with my own local government was probably the most shocking experience. I could almost understand the other government bodies, especially back in Virginia being anti-woman. However, I was not prepared for the utter betrayal I would be served at the offices of the Travis County District Attorney's office. That betrayal to a domestic violence victim pleading for help for her child would not be done just once, but twice. The second time should leave you reeling, sickened, and furious.

Over the years it is hard to imagine what local social service I did not contact. In both the state of Virginia and Texas, I found a consistent lack of care and interest. There was always someone there to answer the phone. Most had staff, but often the offices were not overflowing with women in need. Instead, there is a low-key atmosphere, unnervingly quiet hum.

This odd atmosphere is best exemplified during my visits to the Travis County District Attorney's office where services for victims of domestic violence are located. Even though I expressed an urgency when I called, I was given an appointment to show up several days later.

I went to the appointment with both excited that I was finally going to get the support of a domestic violence advocate and begin the process to seek justice. I sat in the lobby waiting. Watching the quiet office atmosphere quietly humming around the waiting area. Finally, my name was called. I began to feel hopeful at the idea that I was entering a moment where I was going to be officially advocating for another victim of domestic violence. I desperately need someone to step in and help this victim immediately.

The victim was in the midst of an emotional and psychological campaign that had been going over day and night for nearly 30 days. The victim was someone whom I love dearly. I had been the lifeline that was called when she was left alone. I readily admit that I was animated in my explanation of my knowledge of the situation. It is hard not to feel impassioned when you are begging someone with the ability to help. You want to convince them that this urgent. This is really happening. Please help us.

Instead, I was treated with utter disdain. Not only did the "specialist" in front of me tell me to lower my voice, but her colleague next door came over, knocked on the door, and then popped her head in before being asked to enter. The colleague looked at her co-worker with deep concern and asked *her*, "Are you alright? Is everything ok in here?" I sat there speechless. I was sickened to see my tax dollars at work.

Both women who are supposed to be "specialists" to help battered women were offended by my mere speaking of the horrors of domestic violence in their presence. My high sensitivity reading was off the chart for utter contempt. The disdain and repulsion I was treated with were nearly unbearable. I described to my assigned domestic violence specialist all the relevant information I knew. She treated me with a great deal of skepticism and told me there was much she could do because the victim, a Texas resident, was in another state. The specialist coldly ended our appointment. I left the Travis County DA's Domestic Violence office feeling like I had just been punched in the stomach; and all my oxygen had just been extinguished.

The mistreatment and disregard shown to victims of domestic violence are so consistent that I believe it retraumatizes victims. We are gaslighted. They do not believe us because I have not walked through the door with a broken bone protruding from my bloody and battered body.

All these programs, departments, services receive millions of tax dollars every year. It goes first and foremost to the salaries including a full buffet of choices and benefits, paid time off, paid holidays, education reimbursement, and never-ending training.

The issue with training is while I found most of the government employees to offer real help or services, they continue to receive a reliable tax-funded paycheck. Beyond the benefits which easily amount to tens of thousands of dollars, the never-ending training that is built into nearly every organization, is often little more than an excuse to get away from the desk and the family, while continuing to receive that tax-funded paycheck.

Setting up the seemingly never-ending training is one sure way to ensure a never-ending supply of extra tax-dollars. In my opinion, what the government departments have learned is to create and staff the department, but that is all they do. They have people there answering phones, taking names, and addresses and make appointments so they can ultimately log it in on the official rolls that they helped or provided services for many victims. When in fact, they have done little more than wasted my time, treated me with disdain, and pushed me further back from healing. The domestic violence dept director will submit to the taxpayers: Please replenish our budget with a 10% increase. So many victims we want to help but do not have the funds.

Here is an idea: Put a moratorium on training for a couple of years. Victims rarely see the benefits of the never-ending training that most would rather not attend if given the chance. They would rather collect their check from the comfort of their seat in their air-conditioned office. Never do these employees experience what most of the women coming to them for help. The government employee does not live with the fear of being thrown out in the street with her children and nothing more. The mere threat is enough to keep mothers silent and endure abuse. If a victim does manage to escape the horrors of domestic violence, she usually is struggling to find a place to live, feed her children and herself, paid for utilities and necessities. All while staying strong in front of her children, so they are not more afraid than they already are.

Take all the money from all the government budgets and set it aside for a domestic violence victim legal fund. While the employees are sipping tea five comfortable days a week, women and children are scrabbling for food and shelter. Legal representation is luxury few victims can afford. This must change. The system is deeply flawed, and it is time to reform this system and these policies. Women and children must be protected first and foremost.

Austin Police Department: Victim Services

When my life exploded into a legal nightmare, I teetered on hopelessness. Our family abuser had come this far, and no one was willing to stop him. When I received his countersuit stating his intentions of dragging my child back to where he abused both of us, was more than I thought I could handle. I was a walking nervous breakdown. It was nearly impossible to fully function. The thought of losing my child and having her forced to live in hellish existence with our abuser consumed my mind.

As I worked my way down a list of social services and government agencies, I eventually called the Austin Police department. There I found an officer who directed my call to their Victim Services desk. A woman answered and listened as I told her my existence with domestic violence. She was the first decent person whose compassion could be felt over the phone. She counseled me and provided a list of resources. It was the first time I felt I an ounce of hope within the justice system. Over the next 18 months, I would call occasionally. Sometimes for more resources, and sometimes to let her know things were going well because she took the time to genuinely help us.

Jane Do: A Voice of Hope and Guidance

One of the most valuable resources I was provided was a name and phone number. I was given the woman's first name and told to call and leave a message. Explain that I was a domestic violence victim and was assured someone would call back. I made the call and left my message. Within a short amount of time, I received a call. It was a woman who listened to my situation and gave me calm, cool advice. She said I had done so much already, I should go ahead, file out the paperwork and file the case myself. Up until then, I was so exhausted and badged by my abuser, I did not believe I could do it. It would be so hard, so complex. Expensive. I had a list of reasons why I could not do it. The woman on the other end of the line encouraged me to file Pro Se, representing myself.

The Power of One Decent Person

After years of devasting disappointments, I am happy to share that there have been small victories. One of those victories occurred when I was being legally harassed. Having no money, I was glad to fall back on skills gained as an administrator for the City of Henderson Municipal Court.

Henderson is a small town 15 miles outside of Las Vegas. One would normally drive right through on the way to Lake Mead and Hoover Dam. My experience administering the court programs: DUI program and traffic school provided me with invaluable knowledge of the city and court's workings. I also learned how to take a concept like community service and develop it into a cost-saving program that also gave freedom and dignity to the participants. At least 80% chose to perform community service rather than spend a weekend in jail to fulfill their 48-hour commitment. Instead, when given the choice, participants spent several weekends performing outdoor labor and enjoying the benefit of going home each night. The program saved hundreds of thousands of dollars in not housing the participants in jail.

Fast-forward to 2018, when I began getting what I believe was unwarranted legal harassment, I wrote to the court clerk immediately. My hope was the court clerk would be a fair and impartial individual. Some who worked with the citizens of the community.

I explained in my letter to the court clerk how I was a victim of domestic violence and the demands of opposing party was unreasonable. Furthermore, I explained that because opposing party was asking for "any and all material" relating to the situation and to be submitted in ~21 days. In addition to that unreasonable demand, they also demanded I sign a statement that I had handed over EVERYTHING related to the incident that occurred nearly 2 years prior.

I simply asked the court to extend the date so that I could gather the extensive amount of material Michael and his attorney, Francine Meaney, were requesting. I sent my fax and said a prayer.

Ms. Meaney was attorney employed by the Digraceful | Hustle partners. Yes, Judge Judi Disgraceful's husband has a firm. How convenient? Any issue you might have with the court, the judge's husband can fix that for you.

In a town where I could not get an Arlington police officer to take a report on domestic violence/attempted murder, or an attorney referral I could afford as a victim of domestic violence (no money), my abuser used the Fairfax Court system as his personal candy store. Michael Wichael was shopping around and picking up whatever he wanted, as long as he could pay for it. He did it, because he could afford to pay for the official, legal harassment.

Just because he is lobbing legal bombs at me, did not me I had to just lie there and take it. I had written a simple letter asking a simple request.

The next afternoon, my doorbell rang. I had been working in my home office and was dreading another legal bombshell. However, to my delight, I received a letter delivered in person by a processor server—it was official! The letter was from my harasser's attorney. She was thanking the Assistant DA for taking the time to speak with her about the matter. The attorney also confirmed that she had withdrawn all the paperwork and the legal request from court. She also pointed out that I had been notified of the withdrawal.

Wow! You could have knocked me over with a feather. It was one of the few times things did not just go right, they went amazingly well! I was walking on air for weeks! Experiencing a full-fledge smack-down and coming out the victor was an extraordinary experience. I finally had proof of concept that I could affect the specific shade of domestic violence being administered now, legal abuse, and come out the absolute winner.

Even now as I write about this one time when I pushed back against my abuser, I experience a deep and profound sense of accomplishment. I simply used my words and brain to explain what was happening and how seemingly unfair it was.

I asked the court clerk for "an extension", additional time to gather the enormous amount of evidence I had that led up to the incident the attorney was using to harass me. I believe informing the court that I was a domestic abuse victim and my abuser was using this elaborate process just to harass me. The fact was, I pointed out in my letter, the local area police did not bother to anything to the person who had my child barricaded in a second-floor bathroom calling 911 for help. Yet now, the abuser was going to demand all evidence surrounding this incident and drag me into court? I could not afford an attorney and I could not fly to Virginia to even represent myself. I do not know enough about the law to finagle it beyond that. Perhaps some procedure that could have helped me maneuver through what was before me but would require somebody with a law degree.

Eternal gratitude to the fine people who saw that my communication to the court, a simple typewritten letter from my computer, and behaved with clarity, humanity, and ethics. Within 24 hours I was receiving a letter from my abuser's attorney that she had withdrawn the whole thing. The incredible sense of victory I experienced when I read the letter that had been personally delivered to my door was truly a surreal experience. For years, I had been handed defeat after defeat. No help, no services, no respect. Rejection from everyone I turned to for help. Here, for what seemed the first time, was an undeniable victory.

Only now as I write about this deeply personal victory can I begin to appreciate what a crushing blow that was to have an attorney have their asses handed back to them by the District Attorney's office who is ultimately responsible for the legal business of that area. My abuser had to pay for a female attorney to begin a campaign of harassment. Nothing less than a few to several thousands of dollars will get a lawyer to do anything.

I realized that not only did I win big and unexpectedly, my abuser spent thousands of dollars to learn not everyone will go along with his bullshit.

CHAPTER SIX

Is This Really Happening?!

If violence is the salvation of the brutes,
the salvation of man is Justice.

Charles Wagner
French reformed pastor
preface, *Justice*
(1852-1918)

Getting Counter-Sued & Losing My Mind

Unrelenting emotional, verbal, psychological, financial, and legal abuse motivated me to file for Sole Conservatorship (sole custody) in January 2019. After researching, reading, and studying day and night for three weeks, I submitted documents that I carefully prepared for the Travis County District courthouse. They were filled out completely and properly. A court clerk accepted, stamped, and signed my documents. I had them served to the respondent where he would most likely be found—at work.

As amazing as that achievement felt that joy would be incinerated to smithereens when I received the respondent's countersuit. The respondent painted me as an unfit mother who ran an unstable house and was a drug abuser. All unbelievable lies. I did not know you can submit knowingly submit falsehoods to the court. Apparently so.

Fortunately, the claims being made against me were so outrageously false, it was quite easy to disprove with basic evidence. The judge was not happy with what he heard and saw that day. Not only was the countersuit delivering a fatal blow with a "Counter-suit denied." For dessert, the respondent was royally admonished by the judge. It was an unexpected special event to witness from the front row.

The massive cherry on top of this brutal case was the knowledge that the respondent spent tens of thousands of dollars to smear my character in a court room, only to have his ass handed to him and his overpaid, diminutive attorney.

That day in Family Court was absolutely a turning point. My fear evaporated. I was truly winning. As we left the courthouse, we walked victoriously to our car parked directly across the street.

While waiting for my 12-year old car to warm up, we were able to watch our bulbous respondent and his equally hulking honey, squeeze into the back seat of the ride they ordered. We did not need a body language expert to see the respondent was furious. Observing respondent's dash to the rideshare, diving into the back seat, and SLAMMING of the poor driver's door was priceless.

Dancing with Wolves: Attorney Shopping

When I received the Countersuit, the community of advisors I had come to rely on all advised me to hire an attorney. It had become "too complicated".

I dreaded the prospect because of my experience in Virginia. Now I need to shop for an attorney who was licensed in Texas and able to practice in Travis County.

I turned to my list of resources and was eventually given the name of a couple of attorneys. The hearing date was fast approaching. I had managed to avoid dealing with the countersuit until I absolutely had to. Not a good plan and would never advise it, but that is how I coped with this. I just saw the title of the document and never read any further. I knew it would be filled with lies and it was. In my approach, I only had to deal with for about a week instead of the months it had been since it was delivered to my PC.

During one of my visits to the Travis County Law Library, one of the volunteers alerted me of the filing. So, I read it then. I was in hot pursuit to find an attorney. My latest fear would be how would this cost? I had absolutely no money, but I still needed to know: How much will it take for someone to help us?

I called the first number and made an appointment with an attorney. He had an office in a neighboring city. The office was pleasant and so was he. We spoke for the allotted hour of consultation on my case. He charged me $200 for the hour. What I received for that $200 dollars was a bit of an intimidation game (the solid evidence I had would not be admissible; it certainly was) and a referral to another attorney who might be able to help me. The hearing was just days away. Attorneys are ridiculously hard A-type people in general, they do not do spontaneous well.

I called several attorneys who had offices around the downtown courthouse. I figured they were experienced enough to maintain the expensive Austin rent.

I tried to find a female attorney. Someone I hoped who could begin to empathize with me. Time was running out. I did not have time to be choosey, so I called all the numbers referred to me. Most could not consider it because of the short notice. I-began to really lose it: I began freaking out!

I jumped online and did my own search for attorneys in my area that specialized in family law. The hearing was set for just a week away. Rarely have I felt true desperation in my nearly six decades of walking this Earth; this was one of them. I was desperate to find an attorney that could represent me immediately and show up for the hearing schedules in just a few days.

Sharks by the Lake

One of the worst experiences I had shopping for legal representation was when I drove out to the Lake Travis area. This area is considered a better area. Better property. Better views. Everything is supposed to be better. I was hopeful since I had been referred by someone. I was pressed for time and was thrilled they would see me in the morning. That morning I received a call. The attorney I had set the appointment with was not going to be able to make the appointment. He said that I should still go to the office and his partner would take care of me.

I drove out to the lake area and found the office. After getting squared away in a large conference office, I met the other attorney. I explained my situation and showed him the countersuit claims.

The attorney then began what I would call a pathetic shake-down of a victim of violence. I went to the appointment with hopes of hiring a competent, ethical lawyer. Instead, I was told that my case looked "really bad" and that it would be $20,000 *to start*. I explained I only had about $60,000 in equity in my home. I asked if I could lose my home in trying to protect my child. The shmuck coldly replied, "Sometimes that happens."

I thought there had to be some mix-up. He must not have understood how cut and dry this domestic violence situation was. I emailed the original attorney, explained what happened and what was said. The original attorney replied that he firmly stood behind his partner's assessment.

Later I would learn from sources that could trusted, the average child custody case should run about $5,000.

These attorneys had no desire to help a victim. They took glee in driving away any hope I might have of winning or keeping custody of my child. They assumed what my abuser put in his countersuit was true, and based on that false assumption, they saw me as the person portrayed in the countersuit: an unfit, unstable, drug-addicted mother.

I would love to reveal the name of this culprit, but as you can imagine, he would love to beat me in a courtroom.

CHAPTER SEVEN

Thinking Outside the Box

Two roads diverged in a wood,
and I—I took the one less traveled by,
and that has made all the difference.

Robert Frost
American Poet
(1874-1963)

Barred Out & Ghosted in DC

Agency after agency, department after department, all these programs and services designed and funded for the sole purpose of helping victims of domestic violence had failed me. With fierce determination, I went down the list of resources provided to women seeking help. I rarely found the smallest amount of assistance or services. The best services I experienced during my decade-long odyssey came from the non-profits. And when the government agencies failed me, namely the police, CPS, and court systems, I thought about how I might save this sinking ship.

During my research on how to defend against the unrelenting domestic violence we were subjected to, I contacted our abuser's professional organization that allows him to work. The organization's leadership and rules of membership outline their requirements. They also outline the authority to revoked or suspend when membership rules are broken. In my experience, this professional organization has been completely resistant to even acknowledging any items I addressed in my communication with them. For YEARS, they have rebuffed all my efforts to hold their member to their own rules for membership. It should be no surprise that this organization is in Washington DC.

Not sure if the last bit of disgusting disinterest of women and children being abused is that I found a list of "Women in Leadership" on this organization's website. Alongside the glowing description of each woman in leadership with this prestigious organization, it described some of the accomplishments of each woman in leadership. I was thrilled to see that they also provided an email where you could contact these women in leadership. So, I did just that. I emailed approximately a dozen "Women in Leadership". I sat back and hoped to hear from some empowered female voice in leadership.

Perhaps there were some services they could assist me with or point to in at least the right direction. What I heard instead was silence. Complete and utter silence. Not a word. Absolutely nothing. So much for being an empowered woman in a position of leadership. These and women like them, women taking the role to help women, to use your skills, talents, connection, knowledge, or voice and NOT help women, should be removed. Get someone with a voice and a spine. The women's movement for the past 100 years did not endure all that it did so that women like you could just sit on your hands when asked to help.

This organization has a pro bono office. The nasty administrative or one of the Women in Leadership could have *led* me to explore the non-Pro Bono services. But nothing was offered or suggested. No response was made by any woman in leadership. The subject was not important enough to even respond. All that education, and these 'women in leadership' have nothing say except, Go away! We do not care!

Dear Mr. Jefferson

Another government entity that provides our abuser the ability to dodge abusive behavior and still earn money for his specific skills was the United States Patent and Trade Office (USPTO).

My abuser needs authorization from this organization to function as an agent and attorney for this truly historic government institution. Thomas Jefferson is considered the first patent examiner in America.

The USPTO is quite important. It oversees, ordinances, and approves all things related to patents. The detailed rights one has defined and protected by this office. It is a long, administrative process that usually spans years. The patent agents who review the applications are highly specialized in their fields (electronics, biotech, medical, etc.). One needs to study and prepare to pass the test to become a patent agent.

The explicit authorization to prepare patents that will be submitted to the USPTO, as an agent or attorney, is critical. One who works in this field must maintain good standing. I thought this is my US government, not some local program downstream. I will surely receive a positive, supportive response when they see perhaps one of their own golden ones is operating outside the realm of basic human decency. Surely, they will ask him to explain himself. Surely, they will let him know there ought to be no more behavior that generates an impassioned mother begging for help.

I tried not to think about the possible outcomes of the days, then weeks, and months that would drip by. When I did receive a response, it has the usual jargon of denial and unaccountability that I was used to after years of apathy.

One small difference was at the bottom of the letter dated November 29, 2018, was one line, "If criminal charges are filed against Dr. Weichel by a law enforcement agency, or if you have continuing issues with Dr. Weichel's compliance with your divorce agreement, then please do not hesitate to contact OED again."

It felt like I had finally discovered a small crack in the system. This is a path I can pursue. Time would pass as I dealt with more domestic violence and court procedures. Eventually, the time came when I approach the USPTO employee who sent the letter. I explain that this person who operates under the agency's authority was in fact violating a court order as well as basic human decency with family members.

It was a bittersweet experience to receive communication from a staff member. Initially was hopeful because of the things he said and wrote. Ultimately, when the time came to follow through with what he wrote, he would balk.

He dropped the domestic violence ball. He began back-peddling with his support. To add insult to injury, in a phone call around the holidays he delivered a virtual kick to the stomach that completely knocks the wind out of me, "I don't know where you got the idea that I could do anything. I'm just staff." He was in fact, now Chief of Staff.

In the last correspondences, his titled reflected more than "just staff", he was in fact Chief of Staff. The USPTO is made up of mostly attorneys and certified agents. It was heartbreaking after believing for over a year, there was one man in the US government who was not going to swallow the truth and turn a blind eye to domestic violence at its doorsteps. A battered mother begged for help and once again, a government agency did not want to hear it and offered no alternatives.

What is an American mother to do when every US government agency she turns to refuses to acknowledge the violence she and her children are subjected to, often for years? When everyone from the police to CPS to the court system to social services to employers and those who provide memberships and licensing all colludes to do nothing, this is systemic gaslighting. You have been told about abuse and you are deliberately and with full intent, refuse to even acknowledge the victim.

We are denied services beyond the initial "intake interview". I do not believe there is anything behind the curtain. The wizard is pulling levers and staff receive their expected paychecks on a regular basis, all supported with a bountiful buffet of benefits (medical, dental, life, pet, domestic partner), educational reimbursement, paid days off, 12-day holidays minimum, and training—just to name a few things off the top of my head.

I harp on the salaries and benefits because this agency can fight for their existences but do little if anything for victims and their children. We can do better. We can do so much better.

Inform His Employer? It's My Civic Duty

On December 2, 2015, in San Bernardino, California there was a terrorist attack and attempted bombing. Since 9/11, there have been far too many attacks on our American society. What made the December 2015 attack so different was that the news reports stated his wife was involved. Soon stories appeared around her, their marriage, and possible locations. Months later, a similar situation would play out in Florida. Less than a year later, on June 12, 2016, another terrorist attack would befall the Pulse nightclub in Orlando, Florida.

What stood out to me in both tragic events were because the terrorist was married, his wife was under scrutiny until it could be proven she was not involved. Remember, in America "involved" also includes "knowledge" of specific acts, things, etc. This got me thinking that I need to make sure I am not connected or associated with my abuser in any possible way. We were still married, and he had been exhibiting behaviors that were dangerous and unstable. I honestly felt that I had an obligation to inform my abuser's employer of some of the aggressive, destructive, and abusive behaviors we have endured.

Like most entities I have tried to engage with, I did not receive a direct reply or acknowledgment. Luckily for my abuser's childish behaviors, he could not help but complain, and confirm, that my communication with his employer had indeed arrived. Our abuser would complain in exacting detailing what he was called on the carpet for. He would then exaggerate about being on the verge of being fired. He was not exaggerating about being upset and feeling sick to his stomach but being fired was just pure theatrics. He has remained employed and was even promoted as of January 2020, according to the company website. It states that he and five other women were promoted to "Counsel".

Perhaps it was the quality of his work or personality. Perhaps they grew wary of his behavior, rightfully so. For whatever reason, management clearly made the right choice and locked him out of the boys' club. If only I and my children were so lucky as to have that kind of power to protect us from further domestic violence.

The FeMail Campaign

Around August 2018, I created an email campaign. Rather than calling each resource and jump through their hoops to receive no service or help, I decided to use a shotgun approach. I would write an impassioned letter and send it to a list of agencies and individuals I hoped would read my letter and respond. Instead, I was served a huge slice of reality pie. Nobody cares. Of the roughly two dozen packets I sent out, only a few responded. I was most disappointed that I did not receive any type of acknowledge of the packet of information I sent via FedEx to the First Lady of the United States. No response means you do not care.

I hope you, dear reader, are gathering that no one is unreachable. No one is so special that in today's highly connected world, few people are inaccessible. Even more, the information is clearly displayed on some websites. It is in the public domain. If you need to communicate with someone, you can. The information is right there.

The best disinfectant for domestic violence is exposure. Victims by and large live in shame. They do not tell the police. They do not even tell their family and friends. It is this aspect that enables the abuser to continue without fear of anyone finding out what hideous and repulsive behaviors he is inflicting on those closest to him: his family, his "loved" ones. Women and children. The most vulnerable in society are held captive by terror in their own homes by a brutal perpetrator.

The American society asks women living with domestic violence to call for help. That sounds like a great message, but I am here to tell you that is the most shockingly empty statement while offering help. Victims of domestic violence have been living life on the edge for months, and often, years. I believe it is incredibly cruel and further traumatizing when a woman turns to this myriad of programs and services provided through government funding. Departments, divisions, from judges to DA's office to police, there is a steady flow of funds appropriated to help victims of domestic violence. The supervisory and administrative staff get funded. They receive their salaries and benefits—do not get me started. But what is left for the victims? Where are the actual services?

It is though I was looking at this incredibly expensive, yet thin façade. In the front is the signage for support and services but lying just beyond the façade is a fleet of unemphatic bureaucrats who want nothing more than to take your name, address, details, and ask to go away and never come back. Stop asking questions and please take your dreadful life with you.

The Media Blitz

Stopmyabusivehusband@gmail.com was still available

Going it alone was never my desire, but it is what I found I had to do. My abuser is not honoring the divorce decree settlement which states I can request advances. Over the years I asked for money to purchase a safe car. My 12-year-old Honda CRV was on its last leg. With nearly 250,000 miles, I felt it had more than served us. I begged our abuse for any amount to buy a safer car. All requests were met with the iron-fist, authoritarian, "No!". This is the same fascist, literally Fascist, upbringing he complained about growing up in Spain. He was 15 years old when Franco died. The ink was cast.

I was living with someone who knew, experienced, and studied subversive tactics. Mind games the military uses. My abuser provides a new definition of domestic terrorism. My daughters and I lived in absolute terror, every day. This is where even a non-physically abusive environment can still provide a horrifying and traumatizing experience. I think a lot of people dismiss emotional, mental, and psychological abuse. Even the most traumatic abuses, leave NO physical scars, yet the human who has endured this type of abuse is deeply scarred. The abuser has hacked away and hacked away at the victim's self-esteem, self-worth, judgment, behaviors, physical characteristics that little more than a shell of a surviving domestic violence victim exists.

Another wonderful service the internet has provided is an assortment of free programs or apps that allow a person to post videos for free. With all the legwork you have read about, you know I was going to explore a free service I would work on from the comfort of my home.

Full disclosure, I have a degree in communication design and working with many software programs as part of my education. I easily admit that getting on most websites is not as intimidating or complicated as it may be for most. But I am here to tell you that it is by no means rocket science. You do not need to submit any type of paperwork that allows you to get on a website and explore. Read what they have to offer. See how to contact them. Most have a newsletter you can sign up. They want your info and you may want to stay on top of what this organization is doing. At least what they say they are doing.

GoFundMe & the Not-So-Golden Girl

GoFundMe is one of these relatively free websites. This platform allows individuals to raise money for their cause. You can be as descriptive or not as you want. You can post your message, explanation, cause in regular words (text). They also allow you to upload photos.

I got to thinking, since my abuser will not honor the divorce decree and advance me money for an attorney, I can raise money through GoFundMe. Maybe family and friends can help me through that. I wrote my story, explained that I was a victim of domestic violence, and was trying to raise funds for an attorney.

I uploaded photos that I had taken of myself. I had a black-eye, bruises, and scratches around my face and neck. The most horrific and telling image of domestic violence was displayed in the full and completed outline of my abuser's left hand, closed fist. It was just one of the many that landed on my body. This one image is clear. Both in the perpetrator's identity as well as the act of domestic violence.

Still, no one cared. I posted the link to my fund-raiser around the local area. People who should care, first responders, and organizations that ran in the same circles. Over 1,000 people visited my GoFundMe page and not one dollar was donated. They all visited and saw photos of my battered body and plea for help. Not one of these people who live and work in the Washington DC area, one of the most affluent areas of the country, and not one dollar was spared. They saw nothing. They saw no need to help in any way. They came. They look. They saw and just clicked away.

One day I received a surprising notice. Someone had posted to my GoFundMe page. My mind wondered who the compassionate soul was that wanted to reach and help me. I delighted in the chance that perhaps it would be a generous donation and I could go hire an attorney to get me out of the latest legal mess my abuser had me in. Yes, legal abuse is a recognized shade of domestic violence some perpetrators use. Unfortunately for me, my abuser owns stock in this shade.

I checked the website and navigate to my page. I notice my account is flagged. There is a message waiting for me. I am curious. My ad did ask for any pro bono attorney willing to help to contact me. Perhaps it is an attorney wanting to help! I braced myself for possible hate mail or an offer to help. What I did not anticipate was a hate-filled post written by the mother, yes, your good decent people you read this correctly, the mother of Molly Collie.

Are you wondering what this woman, whom I have NEVER met, had to say on my fund-raising page? The page I created to help us against repeated domestic violence, well here you go:

I wished I had captured the entire message, but even here you can get the shade she was sending. I especially love the reference to the "fact" that she believes my abuser has "paid for my education". One, how does she know *anything* about my life? I live 1,500 miles away from this person. I have never met her in my life.

Oh, I know, she often lives with my abuser and her daughter when she stays with Michael and Mollie in the DC area. Latrine Johnson has learned all about me, my life, my schooling, and apparently my finances from my abuser. Obviously, Michael was making public statements about me and the financing of my BFA. Latrine felt confident posting on my fundraising page as those she knew facts. Latrine Johnson has redefined tactless and classless. She has managed to refine a new low. To post such a vile message on a battered woman's fundraiser is beyond the pale. You do not even know me! How many hours have they sat around discussing my life that Latrine felt justified in posting vile, hateful and inaccurate information?

The fundraising page was shut down because the abuser presented lies to his friends at the courthouse. The abuser was handed some assistance to block my page. It has been quite a scene to behold how some government entities enable and support abusive behavior while simultaneously refusing to help a victim of domestic violence when she calls the courthouse begging for help. I will look straight at you, Fairfax County court system.

Venmo & the Big Cry Baby

Years later, with all contacted parties continuing to turn a blind eye, our abuser commits another heinous offense that has now produced a 911 call. With my local DA's office voting thumbs down on helping, I took it upon myself to bring justice by any means possible. I needed help and everywhere I turned, government employees did little more than just take my name and send me a letter stating they were not going to be able to help me. "Budget does not allow…" became the most hated phrase I have ever heard. This is there out. We got our salaries, benefits, and training, sorry victims, we have budgeted NOTHING left for you!

I created my Venmo page. A montage of wedding pictures that led into my battered body and a carousel of legal documents and unflattering emails written by the abuser. All this was sent to the audio the 15-minute recording from a 911 call. My abuser was recorded raging in the background. The caller was begging for help which would take nearly 15 minutes to arrive.

I received little public attention but received a hot, molten lava response from the abuser. He brought me and the Venmo video to the court. He wanted it to stop. At the hearing, the judge pointed out some bad calls on my part in posting the video and ordered me to take down the video. All in all, it was quite painless. When I arrived home that afternoon, I gladly took down my infamous video. The abuser's big nasty countersuit was denied, my child remained in my safe custody, and my confidence was firmly intact.

This was by far my biggest win! The outcome left me utterly elated for weeks. Going home that day and removing the video was not a negative experience. Far from it. I felt victorious! I had my abuser back on his heels. He needed to seek protection from me. This was a new dynamic. There was a time when he counted on me staying quiet. That shame-based victim and era between us had now come and gone. He saw I was clearly willing to expose him. He had to scuttle to hide his recorded rage. His domestic violence.

Did I raise any money? No. Was creating the video harder than creating the GoFundMe page? Yes. The cost of watching my abuser hire an expensive attorney to whine to a judge like a big, legal crybaby: Priceless.

CHAPTER EIGHT

Evolution of a Supernova

As soon as you trust yourself,
you will know how to live.

Johann Wolfgang von Goethe
German writer and statesman
(1749-1832)

Turning Point: Years in the Making

Considering the billions of tax dollars that are direct to fund the police and courthouses and their abundance of tax-funded droids and drones we taxpayers should be questioning: Who are the police and courts really helping?

It sure is not this mother with children who turned to the government agencies numerous times for help. Help for the malignant family abuser who continued to come after my children and me.

Nearly ten years since our escape from his iron-fisted control in Arlington, VA, our abuser still came after us. It took me filing court documents to push this aggressive predator back on his heels.

It may have been the first time my action causes the family abuser to seek his own protection. He needed to hire an attorney to defend his outrageous behavior. There was a lot that needed defending. This turning point took years to materialize, but it made its arrival that much more amazing.

Expanding My Thinking

Part of my education during this odyssey included learning about narcissism and narcissistic abuse. This may not apply to you, but chances are, it might.

I grew up in an era of no internet. When I needed information, I drove to the local library and did research, borrowed books, or spent hours reading at the library. It does not seem that long ago, yet it seems like lightyears when you compare it to the ease and access of information today. We have in our hand's smartphones and personal computers on our desk. Wireless frequency (Wi-Fi) is readily available to most Americans. Whether by phone, PC, or a visit to the public library, many of us can access the internet rather easily.

Although I had internet access, I had little else. Namely, money. I believed I needed money to help me out of my situation. What was limiting me was my thinking. So, I expanded my thinking. I learned new things. I learned about how file documents in the courts acting as my own attorney. I learned more about domestic violence, the family court system, and their procedures and representing yourself in court.

What I did not expect to learn was the hardest truth of all, I had married a highly skilled and malignant narcissist. A highly intelligent and deeply manipulative person who wants to destroy me, my children, our way of life, our happiness.

Apparently, I have been ensnared by the most dangerous type of narcissist, the malignant narcissist. It was not a random entanglement. It was intentional, at least on the abuser's part. My loving parents who never fought or raised their voices in front of us while growing up left me ill-prepared for the real world. Evil does exist and will cross your path at some point. If you are not know told about it, if you are not prepared for it, it will knock you sideways. This is not meant to be funny. Have you ever been T-boned by life that it just left you breathless for weeks or months? Yeah. That is the kind of punch to the gut that I am talking about. As parents, we must do a better job of informing and preparing our children for the real world.

Firing My Attorney

Hiring an attorney in a rush is never a good approach, but it exactly the situation I found myself. However, after the hearing, there was little more than a bunch of emails that came out of badly arranged visitation. No supervised visits with a known abuser. This could never end well, and it did not.

When I asked my attorney what options did, I have, she stated we had to either go to trial or non-suit. Non-suit means to walk away like nothing ever happened. I was nearly five thousand dollars into this procedure. I was assured the four thousand fees would "cover everything" and she would ask for it "at the final hearing". None of that was transpiring. Instead, I was asked for four thousand dollars to go to trial. What?! Why?!

Our abuser had already held a meeting with the court representative and declared his desire to stop all visitation. After years of abuse and filing a countersuit, within 90 days he was waving a white flag. This was never about the child. It was all about domestic violence in the shade of legal abuse. Although he declared no further interest in the fall of 2019, as of this writing he is dragging his feet to bring any resolution. So far, the things I needed for our child and requested through that amazing divorce decree he produced, he has refused all requests to help get his child out of a failing school system.

When I asked the domestic violence counselor where my situation fell on the domestic violence scale. From what she had experienced she also counseled the military during in her career, she said it was one of the worst she had ever heard of. There are far worse cases of physical abuse, this is not what we are referring to. It is the horrific toll that non-physical domestic violence can have on a family. The abuser's intent is to destroy the individual, usually the mother—but children are not spared. This is my situation.

If you are a victim of domestic violence, one idea you might be able to be grateful for is if your abuse is not systemically undermining your parenting or your child directly. The court system is quick to accommodate and facilitate our abuser's experience with the court. While my experience was compounded with the maltreatment of my "parenting class" instructor.

Five weeks of quasi-mandatory attendance. It looks better to the court and judge. Now you may be thinking, "Why, Anna, what could be wrong with parenting classes? We could all learn how to be better parents. What could be the problem?"

I will tell you what the problem is, at least with the Travis County Domestic Relations Office. The department that houses and facilities programs and services for families that need to use the court for protection, peace, or resolution.

My experience with the Parenting program was nothing that I could have prepared for. First, it was 'strongly encouraged' by the court-appointed Guardian ad litum. Her fee was roughly $4,000. The judge ordered me to pay $900 and my countersuit losing abuser paid the rest.

What upset me the most was how the child abuser could literally dial it in. He was court-ordered to take his parenting class over the phone or online. It amounted to hours long, personal calls with a social worker. While my situation was handled like this: I asked for the phone-in class, because the in-person class required that I drive to downtown Austin in the middle of summer where the average temperature is triple digits. The state of Texas has also issued me a disabled placard to accommodate my chronic illness, per my doctor. I brought my disability and request for dial-in classes. Both my attorney and the guardian said no.

So, for the next six weeks, I need to drive into Austin to attended parenting classes taught by the court staff member who will tell you himself that he has been doing this forever. Along with the story of his long association with the program, you will hear in detail his life, his wife, his troubles, and tribulations with life. How this is supposed to make me a better parent is beyond me. It was beyond him too.

The program begins with the new parent to the group starting one day and this parenting class instructor giving a brief introduction and reference to rules and handed a parenting book. Ah, the parenting course workbook. I am sorry, but it is hard for me to not be critical of this workbook. The parenting instructor referred to occasionally while weaving his family stories into every lecture. Never did I leave a lecture feeling or thinking I truly learned something profound or every slightly illuminating on parenting. I learned a lot about this man's life and his family, but nothing on parenting. It was a complete and utter waste of time.

The workbook consisted of little more than a collection of clipart, platitudes, and snippets of parenting advice. The University of Texas is mere miles away from this institution. I am shocked the court has not worked with the eager, brilliant minds of the University to provide or overhaul their "parenting course". Any grad student could produce a wildly more useful "workbook" than what the court has been "teaching" parents for decades.

The "parenting workbook" does little to even being to address or provide useful parenting solutions. The court system is missing a huge opportunity to help families most at need when they fail to provide a basic, useful parenting program when parents are forced to pay this program directly or indirectly. Parents in critical need of help from their government should be getting useful material and providing meaningful information if our attendance is required.

Instead, what I received along a workbook of clipart and platitudes was outright disrespectful. On the first day of the program, the instructor opened the lecture by rubbing a small, polished stone in his hand. He then asked the class which was made up mostly of men. There were about a dozen of us. The instructor announced to a completely silent and attentive class, "Do you know what this is?"

Having been a life-long learner who had spent years in a classroom, I raised my hand. I figured it was a worry stone. A small stone you can carry with you to rub when one feels anxious. Before I could contribute to the "class", this elderly gentleman snapped at me, in front of other adults, "You just want to suck up!" I was left utterly speechless and reeling with embarrassment.

The instructor got exactly what he wanted, for me to shut up. Not to participate or feel welcomed. Just shut up and take it. His lecture continued and he explained how we were in this parenting class, because, "we invited the court into our lives". He crowed about how our inability to parent has now caused the court to teach how to not get in this situation again.

I found out in the next session that there was a primarily women's group. In this class, the same elderly gentleman was much more low-key. No snarky attacks on the audience. Less bravado when telling his family stores which always took up most of the "class". Toward the end, he would briefly mention a page with text on it to remind us that we were in his parenting class and learning how to parent.

On the walls of this windowless conference room, were 8 ½ x 11 pages, sheets of printed pages on the walls. Just in case we did not read those deeply profound platitudes in our "workbook" had not sunken in.

The six-week program ended with the instructor handing out one of the polished stones to the "graduating parents". I felt more like a parent who has served her time. Our abuser was provided with six weeks of personal, one-on-one counseling. He did not have to inconvenience himself by driving to a local parenting class. No, the Travis County court system insisted he did not inconvenience himself. Do not worry about having to leave the comfort and safety of your home. Our abuser did not have to travel or face the eliminates or parking or pay for parking.

No, instead, our abuse was treated to hours of "conversations". That is how he described it to me over a phone call while setting up reunification counseling. If you are required to attend a parenting class, I hope you find yourself in the "right" class.

Prepping the Docs

I had fired my attorney while I came to the conclusion that I would screw up my own case, I should not pay someone else thousands of dollars to not care about my needs and resolution, but instead only cared about milking the situation for all its worth.

Once again, through online research, I came across the concept of the Document Preparer. I knew my case and all the details. I know what I wanted for my child. What I did not know was exactly how to convey that to the court without the opposing party burying me in motions.

I searched online for document preparer, did further research on their reputations, and decided upon one person. I called her and left a message. When she called back, I was standing in the middle of a Home Depot parking lot. On the other end of the line was a confident, knowledgeable female who assured me there was a way out. She said she would prepare all the right documents I needed to file a final order. I felt her fee to be extraordinarily reasonable. Just a few hundred dollars, not thousands.

A lot of time in my child's life has been lost and never to be recovered because of grown adults who are so damaged or incompetent that they undermine my child's basic development and well-being. Government employees who are paid to work on the behalf of a child's best interest are family the child and their families miserably. Because these programs are funded through tax dollars, federal, state, and local, taxpayers must hold these failing institutions to account. They are failing women and children while favoring, accommodating men.

This is institutionalized sex discrimination. It needs to be addressed and overhauled. I wanted the collective majority to come together and demand change. Demand that the old patriarchal favored system be demolished to make way for a new family-favored system. One that protects and defends the vulnerable victims, mother, and child. No longer will the abuser receive preferential treatment in the legal system.

Final Order: Custody Showdown

In Texas, the actual term is not custody, but conservatorship. What it means, at least in my case, I was granted full control over my child's life. I would be able to choose what school, where to live, and most other major decisions without having to consult or receive an agreement with the other parent. I could operate as one, full, and complete parent where decisions for my child. Our abuser had not only continued with his destructive behavior, he created evidence right before the court's eyes. It was so overwhelming; it was hard to hide. I did everything possible to bring it to the court's attention by communicating with the guardian by email and occasionally phone.

On July 20, 2020, my mother's birthday, I sent the final order granting me sole conservatorship to the opposing party's counsel. I felt my parents watching over us from heaven. I waited to see what would transpire.

Since that filing, Mr. Tabacco ignored my email. Three weeks later I sent a "2nd Request" and included some additional and relevant individuals. In my document filed, I stated the truth: Opposing counsel was being unresponsive and I had no hope of him being cooperative. He and his client stated they had no intention of signing the Final Order I had presented to them for review and a signature.

Nothing to fight over. No money. They were choosing to drag out settling a custody issue. This case should have been settled last year. Between Meryl Bowel's games and Wren Tabacco's pedigreed tactics, these officers of the courts ought to be sitting in jail for Contempt of Court. But they won't, because they have an exclusive membership card to 'The Blue Privilege Club'.

I am unable to discuss details of the case. Although multiple pieces of evidence of domestic violence were introduced in court, none of it was addressed by the bench. Rather, I was issued an injunction to take down a video and to not speak to my child about the case.

Just to underscore our abuser's privilege wherever he goes, he violated the injunction numerous times. When I brought this to the attention of our Guardian ad litum, she just blew it off. Our abuser took joy in pointing out that the judge ordered ME to shut up, not HIM. He CC'd our child to remind us that he has an entirely different set of rules he gets to live by.

Last time I was in court, Tabacco was screaming at me that I was a whore and the judge handed over my suicidal daughter right back over to the abuser who had caused her trauma. No supervised visits, nothing special. A dinner meeting was set up, and after a nice meal and a glass of wine, the guardian ad litum left my child with our abuser, at the court's direction. The judge insisted father have a week with the child he voluntarily abandoned for two years.

After the dinner meeting, our abuser spent the next two hours picking at our child's doubts, fears, anxieties, and insecurities. After his 4-hour visit, our abuser wrote a 12-page scathing critique of our child. The child he had just seen for a few hours, after a two-year absence.

He had not sent a birthday or Christmas wishes in years, but he wrote over 5,000 words, criticizing and critiquing the child he sued in court to have access to. What all of us mothers who are victims of domestic violence understand is that this abuser just used the legal system to gain access to his victim, and the court willingly accommodated him.

Our case is on docket for October 7, 2020, 8:30 am. I will post an update at the companion website: www.amc-dvp.com

CHAPTER NINE

Stop Feeding the Monster

Compassion is no substitute for justice.

Rush H. Limbaugh III
Conservative Political Commentator and
2020 Presidential Medal of Freedom Recipient

Civil Servant Incivility: Tax-funded Antagonism

We must demand more of our government. First, we must see these programs and services that are provided through millions and billions of dollars of tax dollars. Those tax dollars come from our pockets. For better or worse, those programs and services are 'our business'. As tax-paying citizens, it is our right and duty to demand more accountability and transparency from our government. I believe programs designed to help victims of domestic violence are not scrutinized and that lack of review and accountability has snowballed into a giant, inefficient headquarter for apathy and antagonism for victims. Victims call or appear for appointments only to be treated with disdain and disrespect. We are asked to tell our stories over and over until we say them without emotion and then are 'not really suffering', it must not have been that bad. I believe that is by design. Keep ignoring this pathetic being and she will eventually go away or stop calling.

No, this can no longer be the business model and motto of domestic violence programs and services across this nation. No longer shall we accept billions of dollars being doled out in the name of helping victims of domestic violence, only to a façade for a non-function, non-producing, non-servicing department. Citizens should demand immediate accountability on what has been accomplished outside funding the staff's retirement while they turn away victims, citizens.

If you are lucky enough to have all that I have described to you as foreign, consider yourself extremely lucky. If, however, you are affected by domestic violence as statistics will sadly state, most of us females will be victims of violence at some point in our life. We all must work and use our majority to change the attitudes of politicians, elected officials, and government workers that the status quo must go. We must gather our economic and political might and demand change.

I want to see reform with the court system to assist and support women to leave violent relationships. Police need a new dynamic. If women are 50% of the population, why is that not reflected in our police forces across the nation? Imagine how interactions with police would differ if half the time you dealt with a woman instead of a man with a badge, poor attitude, and a gun.

Moratorium on Tax-funded Train*cations*

Enough with the damn training! Every department budget for training and seldom does it teach anything. Training seminars benefit trainers and their companies as well as all the tax-funded employees. This additional money should be stopped. I would like to see a moratorium on all training. There is nothing new that police and court staff do not know about domestic violence. But they take time and money each year to leave their desk so they can hang out, have catered breakfast and lunch. If it is over several days, dinner and drinks are included. Yes, how nice for all those government employees exhausted from turning down and turning away victims. I say all that money needs to be donated to a giant domestic violence victims fund to pay for legal representation to ensure a fair divorce and custody arrangement.

First, Take Care of Our Own

One of the primary reasons this book has become a reality is my desire to make significant improvements for the victims of domestic violence. The system in which victims must navigate is complex and can be overwhelming. However, the laws and the people who operate under them create an even greater challenge for victims to overcome. The purpose of this book to shed light, to aim a spotlight on the utter failure of government-funded programs meant to help domestic violence victims.

We must do better by our American sisters and their children. There have been fevered speeches about giving aid and shelter to families, women, and children, but they are from another country. I do not want to hear any American politician speak, demand, that we help non-American citizens over those right here in American that desperately need help. Women who are live in abject fear and anxiety just getting through another day with an unstable, violent man who knows the system works to his advantage and will rarely call him on his abusive behavior.

CHAPTER TEN

America, We Can Do Better

A patriot must always be ready
to defend his country against his government.

Edward Paul Abbey
American author and essayist
(1927 – 1989)

Why Everyone Should Care

Each year, domestic violence costs the US about $6 billion, which is more than the gross profits of all the "Star Wars" movies combined. The U.S. government spends more than $27 billion a year to fight HIV, which affects 1.2 million Americans and spends less than $1 billion on a year to curb domestic violence, which affects more than 46 million Americans.

We call it domestic violence, but what it's really about is what I call malignant misogyny," [9]

---

[9] Mitchell, Jerry. "Most Dangerous Time for Battered Women? When They Leave." *Ledger*, The Clarion-Ledger, 29 Jan. 2017, www.clarionledger.com/story/news/2017/01/28/most-dangerous-time-for-battered-women-is-when-they-leave-jerry-mitchell/96955552/.

Can we all be adults and admit the truth? Our justice system is broken and has been for decades. It's dysfunctionality effects the most vulnerable in society the hardest: women, children, and minorities. Exacerbating the problem further is the dangerous unwritten policy to protect their own: Police, CPS, DA, and Family Court.

America can no longer sit in silence as women and children are brutalized, oppressed, and trapped in their own homes. I believe this is America's most shameful secret: the systemic policy to dismiss domestic violence in general, and specifically if it involves a member employed under the justice department, specifically, the police, CPS, DA, and Family Court.

In my desperate attempt to survive this nightmare, this never-ending series of domestic violence assaults. The various shades of domestic violence used against my children and me. Physical abuse, my photos from August 2010 show a snapshot in time. The black-eye and full outline of his fist imprinted on his wife's flesh tell the story of domestic violence.

Emotional abuse, the relentless assault via text and emails which spew hate, threats, and derogatory insults.

Children are not spared. Sexual abuse, from child molestation to spousal rape, sexual abuse knows no bounds in the world of sexual abuse. Mental abuse, the abuse and ill-treatment of your child by the abuser.

The threat of cutting off all financial support. Mother and child usually existing check to check. This type of threat is easy to throw around and wildly frightening to a mother with children. This introduces financial abuse. Controlling and manipulating family members through control of the family finances. Lastly, and I will admit, this was new to me.

One day I was handed that wheel of violence flier. I commented on how my abuser had shown nearly every description, except one. Legal abuse. Years later, that last unchecked type of control and abuse characteristic was checked off. My abuser had begun assaulting us through the legal system. Filing lies to the courts in Virginia and receiving restraining orders against me (my creative projects online) as well as attempting to harass me where he was the perpetrator. Really? That is what happened when I wrote to the court clerk. I was not the only one pissed with this individual and his tactics. I am forever grateful to the county Assistant District Attorney who stepped in and stopped something wrong from happening.

Experiencing small successes was instrumental in recovering from the depths of my depression. Continued exposure to a threatening and stressful situation can produce a condition beyond PTSD, Post Traumatic Stress Disorder (effects from a single event) to CPTSD (effects from prolonged exposure to trauma), Complex Post-Traumatic Stress Disorder.

This comes from continued and prolonged exposure to events such as domestic violence. The body and mind find ways to cope. Sometimes the results produce immediate ways to cope, but it also postpones and compounds the trauma in responses felt throughout the body. The body processes stress and trauma. The way it displays is both wide-ranging, yet predictable. Why is this? Because women bear the brunt of maintaining the relationship, especially when children are involved.

A. M. CAZARES

The Value of the Life of an American Woman

The National Institute for Justice (NIJ) is a research-based information organization that can help inform policy decisions and improve understanding of the criminal justice system. In a monthly journal they publish, I found a fascinating article that crystalized the disparity in providing any support or relief to victims of domestic violence.

In the NIJ Journal, issue #250, they featured an article which illustrates and underscores the lack of interest and funding to end domestic violence in America. The article, "Borrowing an airline industry strategy-the post-mortem," described commercial airline crashes that draws a great deal of attention. It is shocking to hear about many deaths occurring at once. The following are excerpts from the journal which I found relevant:

The airline industry responds by conducting reviews to find ways to prevent future crashes. Such investigations cost millions of dollars and use enormous amounts of technical expertise. The expensive, sophisticated, and systematic investigation of airline crashes has many benefits, not the least of which are the specific precautions that are subsequently introduced to prevent similar crashes from occurring.

In the United States, deaths traceable to domestic violence are more numerous than those stemming from airline crashes. This raises the question of why comparable amounts of time, money, and expertise are not applied to investigating the causes of domestic violence deaths.

Most domestic violence homicides are not subject to any systematic review, and substantial resources are not spent trying to learn ways to better protect future victims of domestic violence.

Every year in the United States, 1,000 to 1,6000 women die at the hands of their male partners, often after a long, escalating pattern of battering. The estimated number of deaths due to intimate partner violence does not include those women who kill themselves to exit (escape) violent relationships, or who die homeless on the streets avoiding batterers. Like the reviews conducted after an airplane crash, a fatality review helps determine what went wrong and what could have been done differently to prevent the tragedy. It is a fatality review.

In a fatality review, community practitioners and service providers identify homicides and suicides resulting from domestic violence, examine the events leading up to the death, identify gaps in service delivery, and improve preventive interventions.

The review team asks many questions: Did the victim approach a social service or law enforcement agency? If so, what services and interventions were provided? How might these have been provided more effectively? How might the victim have been better protected?

In short, a fatality review identifies relevant social, economic, and policy realities that compromise the safety of battered women and their children.

Reviewing domestic violence deaths over time might identify broader issues with social policies, criminal justice intervention strategies, and political initiatives.[10]

---

[10] Websdale, Neil. "Borrowing an Airline Industry Strategy." *NIJ Journal - Reviewing Domestic Violence Deaths*, vol. 250, Nov. 2003, pp. 27–28.

I wonder if you are as enraged as I am reading about how the airline industry pours extraordinary amounts of money into preventing future airline crashes, but only a tiny fraction is devoted by our government toward ending domestic violence.

Blue Privilege: Peace and Justice Denied

Blue Privilege is what the "thin blue line" has graduated to: a privilege. It went from an attitude and culture of protecting each other to now it is a pervasive, institutionalized process of protecting their own.

It is safe to say across the board that rejection and denial are difficult to face and deal with. Try to imagine how to deal with rejection and denial when you are calling the police, CPS, or family court for help. Help from an abuser. Help to protect your children. This should not be happening in American in 2020, but it is.

My experience over the past decade has been complete and utter rejection and denial of the helping I desperately needed as well as the abuse we were forced to endure because the US government agencies funded by US taxpayers, did not do their job. They stand erect in their hardened exteriors. These monoliths of cold, hard marble which stand in our cities house cold, hard employees who are paid handsomely.

Before any of those same government employees pipe up and try to begin explaining how they are not "getting rich", they will claim they are taking a pay cut "to serve the people". Here is a great test: Let those same government employees find themselves unemployed. Without the bountiful government benefits.

Let these same ineffective and resentful employees go find a job in the real world and experience that comparable pay without the security that government jobs have. Let these same rude and indifferent government employees get through an interview and land the job with their cold and harden exterior. I highly doubt it. Because any business owner who has dealt with government employees understands that this the apex of averageness, mediocrity, and complacency.

Using Our Majority for Meaningful Change

White American women gained the right to vote in 1920, but it would be nearly half a century, before Black American women were would be given the right to vote on August 6, 1965.

Currently, women make up 50.8% of the American population.[11] The historic episode in our American history came about by when the unempowered decided to come together for a righteous and worthy cause.

By earning the right vote, women also gained the ability to own land, start a business, and vote on issues that affect her life and property. An extraordinary accomplishment that most women today do not think about. Gaining the right to vote came from women coming together and supporting an enormously worthy cause.

---

[11] "U.S. Census Bureau QuickFacts: United States." *US Census Bureau*, 2018, www.census.gov/quickfacts/fact/table/US/HSG445218.

Make no mistake, men did not want to share in the power. Men fought viciously against the suggested change to the male-dominated system. The progressive women persevered and history was made on August 18, 1920.

Exactly 100 years have passed since that extraordinary act of congress was passed. Yes, many things have improved for women. However, one thing has remained a constant: domestic violence

Women have done much with gaining the right to vote. The right to vote means participating in a system that has direct effects on one's life. From owning property or a business to paying taxes or working for others. Any significant right or business is affected by voting. Women must participate in the system every time. We cannot any gains made over the past 100 years, slip away due to ignorance or laziness.

American women have made advances in economic terms. Combined with easily being the majority in the workforce, women who own property in the US is 12.7%.[12] Women are also creating work for themselves and others. The number of women-owned businesses is 11.6 million.[13]E

Yet, we need to remember there are still women who have not gained true freedom. These women are trapped in a violent and oppressive

---

[12] "2019 Statistics on Women and Women's Homeownership." *NAWRB*, Women in Housing Ecosystem Report, 2019, www.nawrb.com/community/statistics-on-women-and-home-ownership/.

[13] "Resources." *NAWBO*, National Association of Women Business Owners, 2019, www.nawbo.org/resources/women-business-owner-statistics.

relationship. Worst of all, the victims of domestic violence are trapped in their homes with their children.

American women cannot continue to go to work or school as though all is perfect. We must come together and demand, yes demand, better treatment, and services for our society's most vulnerable. I would argue our most valued members of society: those who bring life into the world and the new lives.

Where will our society be if we all violent men to terror mothers and children in their homes? Home is supposed to be our sanctuary from life. A place where you can let down your guard and relax.

But when that home is occupied by an abuser, the house is filled with unpredictable violence. The house feels like a prison and there is only one, violent guard on duty.

The driving force behind this book is to explain to America what happens when that mother turns to the police for help, or to be more accurate, what does not happen when a victim of domestic violence calls for help—to any of these government agencies. Nothing. That is what I found. Nothing is done to the abuser. Nothing but the runaround is given. Nothing but cold rejection is served up consistently by these well-paid, fully benefited, and allegedly well-trained government employees.

CHAPTER ELEVEN

A National Call to Action

Until the great mass of the people shall be filled with the sense of responsibility for each other's welfare, social justice can never be attained.

Helen Keller
American author, activist, and lecturer
First deaf-blind person to earn a Bachelor of Arts degree
(1880-1968)

Fast-tracking Justice: An Army of Attorneys

As a survivor of the horrors of domestic violence, the one thing I was in search of was freedom. Freedom from the abuse. Freedom from the daily fear and anxiety that wears a soul down. Exhausted and beaten, I went from office to office and agency to agency. All were occupied with staff and running utilities.

It always struck me as odd, that there could be a tremendous amount of turmoil happening in a victim's life, the reason these offices exist. The abuser could be turning the life of the victim upside down and inside out with obsessive, repetitive, vulgar, or hateful email, text, and phone harassment. When the abuser is not beating, strangling, or raping his intimate partner, the abuser may be inflicting emotional and psychological abuse by using women's children or threatening to harm them.

The administrative staff just reflexively process you like you were there merely to pick up a parking sticker. Not the fact that you are sitting in the lobby of the police, CPS, or DA's office praying for protection and peace from your abuser. Praying for the living nightmare that has become your daily existence. Living with every shade of domestic violence all at once.

Time after time I left each appointment or office, empty-handed and unprotected from our abuser. I was no better off than when I arrived. It is absolutely disgraceful that billions of dollars are spent on programs directed to help women and children escaping domestic violence but are undermined by the police officer who will not take a report or act on child abuse. When CPS dismisses the abused child and accommodates the adult. Where does a battered woman turn when the District Attorney's office refuses to protect an abused child in order to protect a fellow attorney's career?

America, we have no one to blame but ourselves. We have allowed the government and its politicians to become more important than its citizens. American has lost sight of protecting the basic rights, safety, and dignity of its most vulnerable citizens: women and children.

Women and children trapped and oppressed by domestic violence should not have to pay thousands of dollars to escape their tormentor.

A simple solution would be to have a massive Pro Bono attorney campaign. The US Justice Department is the cause of much of this abuse and violence to continue in the lives of American women and children. It should be their top priority to immediately address this gross violation of human rights!

The actual paperwork involved in a simple separation, divorce, or child custody is minimal. The majority of the document is already preprinted, and spaces left blank to insert names of parents and the child. Even minor modification to visitation is easily accomplished with the use of computer software to update the forms.

My position is the US Justice system, and the attorneys who operate within it, are profiting from the horrific experiences of women and children trapped and oppressed by domestic violence. These government departments and agencies submit budgets each year, under the pretense of helping battered women and children. The unmet needs of millions of victims paint a truer picture. Victims are denied services and protection from the police to the US Supreme Court.

One way to address domestic violence in a sweeping and meaningful way is to provide unlimited legal services to American victims of domestic violence. Allow them the ability to leave their captors, their tormentors, their rapists, their abusers.

Provide a nationwide program for victims to call an 800 number and submit their name and contact information. A law firm or attorney should contact the victim and begin the process of freeing her from violence. More complicated cases should be spread among large law firms who can afford to absorb the costs. Women and children have been brutalized by their abuser and the system. We can no longer accept a wildly dysfunctional system. We must demand change. Until the Department of

Women is in place, the US Justice Department and the supporting legal industry need to cover all the costs involved in righting this historic wrong.

The American Justice system is broken and failing women and children. I do not see an urgent call from our government or political leaders to change the existing system. Therefore, I call on my American sisters and brothers to unite against the system which supports abusive men. I am asking each of us to petition our government to change, to demand a Department of Women to oversee the protection and policy which improve the lives of American women and children.

If we see no response or genuine interest in our government, I further encourage my fellow American's to take our story of neglect and abuse at the hands of the US Justice Department, and petition the United Nations, Status of Women.

Put the international spotlight on the US government's lack of interest in address the problems victims face. Americans must be made aware that domestic violence is a human rights violation. We must not allow our government to be so complacent or to collude in undermining the safety and well-being of American women and children.

The attorneys for Jessica (Gonzales) Lenahan took their case to the UN when the US Supreme Court ruled against the victim and announced police can just use their own judgment when it comes to enforcing those what are they called, oh yeah, protection orders issued by the police. It seems writing your shopping list on the back of that paper would probably provide a victim of domestic violence more use than the words printed on the other side. Just words, no guarantee of protection.

Fast-tracking Freedom: Housing & Jobs

One of the first things any mother needs is to secure shelter for her and her children. Fast-tracking freedom for victims of domestic violence begins with providing immediate, affordable housing.

With all of the economic disruption from the COVID19 pandemic, there will be an abundance of multi-unit properties. If the US government wanted to quickly house refugees, it would send in the Army of Engineers and quickly put together a plan and successfully execute it. Why can't our government focus on getting massive housing set up for women and their children who are forced to exist each day in America, living in fear and anxiety?

If housing were set up in a hotel, simple marketable skills would easily be trained and transferred to the adult residents. As part of their contribution, they would be learning hospitality and culinary skills. Probably the most important factor would be living with other survivors, so they do not feel like a pariah in society. Living in a communal setting before transitioning to independent living would provide easier access to much-needed counseling services for mothers and their children.

What if we take basic needs and really apply our American resources to help those who have neglected by their partners and their government. Allow ourselves to imagine designing a recovery center for women and children who are escaping domestic violence, a Freedom Center. It might look something like this:

The center would need to be accessible for women in the area, yet set in large, open, fertile land. There, a residential farmhouse for women and their children to make the extraordinary transition from being trapped as a dependent in a violent relationship to be an independent, woman with marketable skills and a job opportunity.

Normally, domestic violence shelters allow for a 30 day stay. This 30-day countdown to being kicked out is hardly a welcoming situation. In an ideal center for women who want to truly escape being a victim and a dependent in a domestic violence situation, women and their children would be given up to one year to make the transition.

Currently, the 30-days is barely enough to get your head focused enough to deal with any immediate police, CPS, or court appointments. I believe victims escaping the horrors of domestic violence need time to adjust to freedom.

At this ideal center along with the residential center where the women and children live, sleep, and house their belongings, there will be two more supporting facilities. One could be a one-room schoolhouse or a creative approach to do more with a less traditional school setting. Children would be able to keep up with their schoolwork as well as creating familiar structure to their day. The much need predictability of school.

Providing consistent and nutritious meals three times a day to the women and children will contribute to their health and overall healing. Accessing funds through local food stamp programs could easily make this possible. The training and commodore among the residents provide structure, meal sharing, and the organized preparation of healthy, affordable foods to that when the women leave, they are more prepared to successfully and skillfully shop and prepare nutritious meals on a realistic budget.

The last facility I envision being on this property would be a combination counseling and training center. Being able to provide easy access to highly focused counseling would provide enormous support and motivation for women to deal with multi-faceted aspect of domestic violence.

A woman escaping a domestic violence home needs to find a new, safe place to live. She will likely have children with her. I believe one of the grossest miscarriages of justice and humanity that government employees commit when they treat victims seeking service with disdain and indifference is that what they are being paid for is to help domestic violence victims. The words themselves describe a human who was trapped, exploited, and abused. The experience would leave anyone traumatized. The effects of this trauma vary from victim to victim and how they internalize and process, or not, the horrors they were subjected to.

This is a person who has and is experiencing trauma and the last they think they need to be jerked around by a system, departments, and their nicely paid staff. Victims do not need to show up to appointments that do not amount to any help. Our information is spread from agency to agency. Each of advocates not for the victim, but for another agency to receive another statistic.

Services do not have to materialize; the point is to get your name and all the details of what happened. This information will get files and lost. The victim is asked to refile. Wearing down the victim is part of their business model, apparently.

If the domestic violence programs and services can report all these women who came to the office for help. Look, we need to keep that funding rolling in, maybe even increase it 10% while you are at it.

What needs to change is full transparency and accountability. There needs to be a type of annual report that shows all that has been accomplished from the funding and made public. This should be as anticipated as the consumer reports on your favorite car. This report would tell us taxpayers who effectively these programs and services are delivering. Not just showing up for coffee, tea, and leave by three. No, we want to see tangible results, not just your staff's paystubs.

A Freedom Center would house counseling and job training facilities. Both specialized counseling and job training are essential to enable former victims for a new life. A life with their experiences guided to recovery. A life with a clear path to earning a living. Both components are necessary to achieve true freedom.

Imagine a big gorgeous farmhouse designed by Joanna Gaines with all the warmth and comfort victims need. Imagine a lovely garden that provides fresh vegetables for each meal. Women would be taught how to grow their own affordable and nutritious food. Imagine the children being able to take part in preparing the soil and experience the miracle of planting a single seed. Imagine what the women and children would learn, experience, and gain from watching their labor produce delicious, beautiful food from the ground, water, and sun. Tending to the garden remind each garden that we need to also tend to ourselves to grow stronger every day. Imagine giving victims who have escaped a brutal existence a new lease on life, an opportunity to heal, grow, and succeed.

I understand 30 days in a shelter is an enormous gift for many women. However, we must do more. We must do much, much more. Thirty days is not nearly enough. Most of the shelters are funded through grants and government funding.

The Erosion of Public Trust

I believe the best research and writing has already been performed. I would like you simply present the findings from the Pew Research Center, a nonpartisan American think tank based in Washington, D.C. It provides information on social issues, public opinion, and demographic trends shaping the United States and the world. The following are excerpts I found relevant to domestic violence:

> *Many Americans see declining levels of trust in the country, whether it is their confidence in the federal government and elected officials or their trust of each other. Most believe that the interplay between the trust issues in the public and the interpersonal sphere has made it harder to solve some of the country's problems.*

> *Three-quarters of Americans say that their fellow citizens' trust in the federal government has been shrinking and 64% believe that about peoples' trust in each other.*

Americans are making the connection between what they think is poor government performance, especially gridlock in Washington, and the toll it has taken on their fellow citizens' hearts. Overall, 49% of adults think interpersonal trust has been tailing off because people are less reliable than they used to be.

Americans see distrust as a factor inciting or amplifying other issues, they consider crucial. For example, in their open-ended written answers to questions, some Americans say they think there are direct connections between rising distrust and other trends they perceived as major problems, such as partisan paralysis in government, the outsize influence of lobbyists and moneyed interests, confusion arising from made-up news and information, declining ethics in government, the intractability of immigration and climate debates, rising health care costs and a widening gap between the rich and the poor.[14]

The need to restore trust in our government applies to all in the US government. However, it is my position that the erosion of trust and proof that women and children do not receive the same rights and protections under the US Constitution when it comes to escaping domestic violence in America.

From the police officer who refuses to help a mother file a police report about the abuse, she has suffered to the US Supreme Court shredding any

[14] Rainie, Lee, and Andrew Perrin. "Key Findings about Americans' Declining Trust in Government and Each Other." Pew Research Center, 22 July 2019,www.pewresearch.org/fact-tank/2019/07/22/ key-findings-about-americans-declining-trust-in-government-and-each-other/.

hope of protection when it announced Protection Ordered issued by the police are to be enforced ONLY at the police's discretion.

All this is completely unacceptable. If American women cannot confidently rely on the police, CPS, DA's office, or Family Court to protect her and her children from abusive men, we must find a new solution. The old system is purposely broken and designed to protect abusive men. Men support this system. It works for them.

I want to remind my fellow Americans that women have a slight majority in the population, but a majority it is. We, American sisters, need to unite and demand a radical change to the system that effects women's lives. I have no intention of putting a bandage on a gushing wound across the heart of American women. No longer should we settle for small offices here or there, at the bottom of the US Justice Department structure.

I say we need to create a new Cabinet-level department, the Department of Women. Women have a unique existence in that our bodies perform in a way to allows for birth. This occurs over a span of approximately 20 years. There are several extraordinary health issues that are unique to a woman's existence. In addition to these challenges, women often must travel through life while caring for additional humans, their children. The enormous load of responsibility that the American government and American men place on women, especially mothers, has gone on for too long.

The nightmarish experience I have endured over the past 10 years due to the US Justice Department's policies toward women, written and especially the unwritten policy of Blue Privilege, have left me with no alternative solution, but to walk away from a wholly ineffective system.

American women should demand a department of their own. Included in there would be a division for children. We should be encouraging our children to participate in our democracy, not at 18, but be engaged from childhood. How might we improve the lives of our children if they were provided a mode, website, and 800 number, to report their concerns? The two biggest areas would be home life and school. How might we be able to address the real concerns of our children if we had the courage to allow them to speak freely?

Cabinet departments are headed by a Secretary who sits on the President's Cabinet. Secretaries are responsible for directing the de4partment's policy and for overseeing its operation. Each department has a special area of policy, although their responsibilities are still very broad. The organization of each it's quite complex, but they have some things in common. All Secretaries have a Deputy or Undersecretary, as well as a host of Assistant Secretaries. Most departments are divided into bureaus, divisions, and sections.[15]

A Department of Women would house all the programs that are scattered throughout the government. To concentrate related programs under a single cabinet-level department would be tremendous attention, power, and funding for future programs and services. Issues such as changes to the family law code to address financial and legal abuse could be created and applied nationwide. Also, the remove unfair child support laws.

---

[15] "The Organization of the Bureaucracy." *Ushistory.org*, Independence Hall Association, 1 Aug. 2020, www.ushistory.org/gov/8b.asp.

The current judicial apparatus demands oversight as well as serious review and reform of their agencies' policies toward the treatment of women.

- ✓ Reform Police Policies

- ✓ Reform CPS process

- ✓ Reform DA office process & victim treatment

- ✓ Reform Family Court process

Severe punishments should befall employees of the US Justice Department (police, CPS, DA and Family Court and peripheral agencies and family law industry) who betray the public's trust.

Justice shall not be delayed, diverted, or denied. To do so is a direct violation of a citizen's constitutionally protected rights. Once a report has been filed by a spouse, child, or partner of a government agency, any further abuse will constitute immediate termination and loss of any benefits.

Justice Scalia's decision to announce to the police that they can "use their discretion" when it came to enforce a Court issued Protection Order. The justice's decision came when an Arizona mother and victim of domestic violence was granted a Protection Order. The subject was her abusive husband and father of her three young children.

On June 5, 1999, around 5:30 pm, the children's father stopped by and took all the kids up from the front yard and then left. He never communicated with the mother about any of his plans or intentions. She knew nothing about where her children were, except for the fact that they were with her abusive husband.

The mother, Jessica (Gonzales) Lenahan, had contacted the police numerous times begging them to do find her children; to enforce the protection order. By Sunday night, the mother was frantic and getting absolutely no support from the Castlerock, Colorado police.

"At approximately 3:20 a.m., respondent's husband arrived at the police station and opened fire with a semiautomatic handgun he had purchased earlier that evening. Police shot back, killing him. Inside the cab of his pickup truck, they found the bodies of all three daughters, whom he had already murdered."[16]

This horrific example of domestic violence illustrates and punctuates, that from the police to the US Supreme Court, domestic violence victims cannot count on anyone or anything in America for protection from domestic violence.

If any help is extended, be grateful, because a man sitting on the highest seat in the country, judged, decided, and wrote that a Protection Order is only as enforceable as the police say it is. From top to bottom and back again, women and children are left defenseless in America.

It is a bittersweet task to write about the dissenting minority opinion, those who opposed the majority, because to me it seems the obvious was once again the men, and a few women, at the top of the Justice Department, the US Supreme Court, contorted his legal tongue to make the most obscure legal argument--that won.

[16] Scalia, Antonin G. "Castle Rock v. Gonzales, 545 U.S. 748 (2005)." *Justia Law*, US Supreme Court, 5 June 2005, supreme.justia.com/cases/federal/us/545/748/.

Now listen to the reasoning of the minority opinion. The justice who did not see the Castlerock case through wife-beater sunglasses, but instead wore no eyewear on at all. Justice Stevens saw perfectly clear in 2005.

Too bad the majority of the justices did not agree. There have been a few times over the past 10 when I felt anyone, especially in our government, to be in my corner.

I do not understand all the legal details of Justice Stevens dissenting opinion, but what I do understand is that he saw what victims understand: we turn to the police for help and protection. If you refuse, we are left vulnerable and helpless. That should not be happening in America in 2020, but it is.

I have included Justice Stevens' dissenting opinion in its entirety to honor the man and his clear vision of the simplicity of right and wrong, especially when it came to protecting society's most vulnerable. He did not need to make extraordinarily complex legal arguments to make his point. Instead, Justice Stevens wrote with clarity, conviction, and a common sense that is easy for us to understand:

STEVENS, J., DISSENTING
CASTLE ROCK V. GONZALES
545 U. S. _____ (2005)
SUPREME COURT OF THE UNITED STATES
NO. 04-278

TOWN OF CASTLE ROCK, COLORADO, PETITIONER *v.* JESSICA GONZALES, individually and as next best friend of her deceased minor children, REBECCA GONZALES, KATHERYN GONZALES, and LESLIE GONZALES on writ of certiorari to the united states court of appeals for the tenth circuit [June 27, 2005]

Justice Stevens, with whom Justice Ginsburg joins, dissenting.

The issue presented to us is much narrower than is suggested by the far-ranging arguments of the parties and their *amici*. Neither the tragic facts of the case, nor the importance of according proper deference to law enforcement professionals, should divert our attention from that issue. That issue is whether the restraining order entered by the Colorado trial court on June 4, 1999, created a "property" interest that is protected from arbitrary deprivation by the Due Process Clause of the Fourteenth Amendment.

It is perfectly clear, on the one hand, that neither the Federal Constitution itself, nor any federal statute, granted respondent or her children any individual entitlement to police protection. See *DeShaney* v. *Winnebago County Dept. of Social Servs.*, 489 U. S. 189 (1989). Nor, I assume, does any Colorado statute create any such entitlement for the ordinary citizen. On the other hand, it is equally clear that federal law imposes no impediment to the creation of such an entitlement by Colorado law. Respondent certainly could have entered into a contract with a private security firm, obligating the firm to provide protection to respondent's family; respondent's interest in such a contract would unquestionably constitute "property" within the meaning of the Due Process Clause. If a Colorado statute enacted for her benefit, or a valid order entered by a Colorado judge, created the functional equivalent of such a private contract by granting respondent an entitlement to mandatory individual protection by the local police force, that state-created right would also qualify as "property" entitled to constitutional protection.

I do not understand the majority to rule out the foregoing propositions, although it does express doubts. See *ante*, at 17

("[I]t is by no means clear that an individual entitlement to enforcement of a restraining order could constitute a 'property' interest"). Moreover, the majority does not contest, see *ante*, at 18, that if respondent did have a cognizable property interest in this case, the deprivation of that interest violated due process. As the Court notes, respondent has alleged that she presented the police with a copy of the restraining order issued by the Colorado court and requested that it be enforced. *Ante*, at 2, n. 1. In response, she contends, the officers effectively ignored her. If these allegations are true, a federal statute, Rev. Stat. §1979, 42 U. S. C. §1983, provides her with a remedy against the petitioner, even if Colorado law does not. See *Cleveland Bd. of Ed.* v. *Loudermill*, 470 U. S. 532 (1985).

The central question in this case is therefore whether, as a matter of Colorado law, respondent had a right to police assistance comparable to the right she would have possessed to any other service the government or a private firm might have undertaken to provide. See *Board of Regents of State Colleges* v. *Roth,* 408 U. S. 564, 577 (1972) ("Property interests, of course, are not created by the Constitution. Rather, they are created and their dimensions are defined by existing rules or understandings that stem from an independent source such as state law—rules or understandings that secure certain benefits and that support claims of entitlement to those benefits").

There was a time when our tradition of judicial restraint would have led this Court to defer to the judgment of more qualified tribunals in seeking the correct answer to that difficult question of Colorado law. Unfortunately, although the majority properly identifies the "central state-law question" in this case as "whether Colorado law gave respondent a right to police enforcement of the restraining order," *ante,* at 8, it has chosen to ignore our settled practice by providing its *own* answer to that question.

Before identifying the flaws in the Court's ruling on the merits, I shall briefly comment on our past practice.

I

The majority's decision to plunge ahead with its own analysis of Colorado law imprudently departs from this Court's longstanding policy of paying "deference [to] the views of a federal court as to the law of a State within its jurisdiction." *Phillips* v. *Washington Legal Foundation*, 524 U. S. 156, 167 (1998); see also *Bishop* v. *Wood*, 426 U. S. 341, 346, and n. 10 (1976) (collecting cases). This policy is not only efficient, but it reflects "our belief that district courts and courts of appeal are better schooled in and more able to interpret the laws of their respective States." *Brockett* v. *Spokane Arcades, Inc.,* 472 U. S. 491, 500–501 (1985); *Hillsborough* v. *Cromwell*, 326 U. S. 620, 629–630 (1946) (endorsing "great deference to the views of the judges of those courts 'who are familiar with the intricacies and trends of local law and practice' "). Accordingly, we have declined to show deference only in rare cases in which the court of appeal's resolution of state law was "clearly wrong" or otherwise seriously deficient. See *Brockett*, 472 U. S., at 500, n. 9; accord, *Leavitt* v. *Jane L.*, 518 U. S. 137, 145 (1996) *(per curiam)*.

Unfortunately, the Court does not even attempt to demonstrate that the six-judge en banc majority was "clearly wrong" in its interpretation of Colorado's domestic restraining order statute; nor could such a showing be made. For it is certainly *plausible* to construe "*shall* use every reasonable means to enforce a restraining order" and "*shall* arrest," Colo. Rev. Stat. §§18–6–803.5(3)(a)–(b) (Lexis 1999) (emphases added), as conveying mandatory directives to the police, particularly when the same statute, at other times, tellingly employs different language that suggests police discretion, see §18–6–803.5(6)(a) ("A peace

officer *is authorized to* use every reasonable means to protect
…"; "Such peace officer *may* transport …" (emphases
added)).[Footnote 1] Moreover, unlike today's decision, the
Court of Appeals was attentive to the legislative history of the
statute, focusing on a statement by the statute's sponsor in the
Colorado House, *ante,* at 10, n. 6 (quoting statement), which it
took to "emphasiz[e] the importance of the police's mandatory
enforcement of domestic restraining orders." 366 F. 3d 1093,
1107 (CA10 2004) (en banc). Far from overlooking the
traditional presumption of police discretion, then, the Court of
Appeals' diligent analysis of the statute's text, purpose, and
history led it to conclude that the Colorado Legislature intended
precisely to abrogate that presumption in the specific context of
domestic restraining orders. That conclusion is eminently
reasonable and, I believe, worthy of our deference.[Footnote 2]

II

Even if the Court had good reason to doubt the Court of
Appeals' determination of state law, it would, in my judgment, be
a far wiser course to certify the question to the Colorado Supreme
Court.[Footnote 3] Powerful considerations support certification
in this case. First, principles of federalism and comity favor
giving a State's high court the opportunity to answer important
questions of state law, particularly when those questions
implicate uniquely local matters such as law enforcement and
might well require the weighing of policy considerations for their
correct resolution.[Footnote 4] See *Elkins* v. *Moreno*, 435 U. S.
647, 662, n. 16 (1978) (*sua sponte* certifying a question of state
law because it is "one in which state governments have the
highest interest"); cf. *Arizonans for Official English* v. *Arizona*,
520 U. S. 43, 77 (1997) ("Through certification of novel or
unsettled questions of state law for authoritative answers by a
State's highest court, a federal court may save 'time, energy, and
resources, and hel[p] build a cooperative judicial federalism' "

(brackets in original)).[Footnote 5] Second, by certifying a potentially dispositive state-law issue, the Court would adhere to its wise policy of avoiding the unnecessary adjudication of difficult questions of constitutional law. See *Elkins*, 435 U. S., at 661–662 (citing constitutional avoidance as a factor supporting certification). Third, certification would promote both judicial economy and fairness to the parties. After all, the Colorado Supreme Court is the ultimate authority on the meaning of Colorado law, and if in later litigation it should disagree with this Court's provisional state-law holding, our efforts will have been wasted and respondent will have been deprived of the opportunity to have her claims heard under the authoritative view of Colorado law. The unique facts of this case only serve to emphasize the importance of employing a procedure that will provide the correct answer to the central question of state law. See *Brockett*, 472 U. S., at 510 (O'Connor, J., concurring) ("Speculation by a federal court about the meaning of a state statute in the absence of a prior state court adjudication is particularly gratuitous when, as is the case here, the state courts stand willing to address questions of state law on certification from a federal court").[Footnote 6]

III

Three flaws in the Court's rather superficial analysis of the merits highlight the unwisdom of its decision to answer the state-law question *de novo*. First, the Court places undue weight on the various statutes throughout the country that seemingly mandate police enforcement but are generally understood to preserve police discretion. As a result, the Court gives short shrift to the unique case of "mandatory arrest" statutes in the domestic violence context; States passed a wave of these statutes in the 1980's and 1990's with the unmistakable goal of eliminating police discretion in this area. Second, the Court's formalistic analysis fails to take seriously the fact that the Colorado statute at issue in this case was enacted for the benefit of the narrow class of persons who are beneficiaries of domestic restraining orders, and that the order at issue in this case was specifically intended to provide protection to respondent and her children. Finally, the Court is simply wrong to assert that a citizen's interest in the government's commitment to provide police enforcement in certain defined circumstances does not resemble any "traditional conception of property," *ante*, at 17; in fact, a citizen's property interest in such a commitment is just as concrete and worthy of protection as her interest in any other important service the government or a private firm has undertaken to provide.

In 1994, the Colorado General Assembly passed omnibus legislation targeting domestic violence. The part of the legislation at issue in this case mandates enforcement of a domestic restraining order upon probable cause of a violation, §18–6–803.5(3), while another part directs that police officers "shall, without undue delay, arrest" a suspect upon "probable cause to believe that a crime or offense of domestic violence has been committed," §18–6–803.6(1).[Footnote 7] In adopting this legislation, the Colorado General Assembly joined a nationwide movement of States that took aim at the crisis of police underenforcement in the domestic violence sphere by implementing "mandatory arrest" statutes. The crisis of underenforcement had various causes, not least of which was the perception by police departments and police officers that domestic violence was a private, "family" matter and that arrest was to be used as a last resort. Sack, Battered Women and the State: The Struggle for the Future of Domestic Violence Policy, 2004 Wis. L. Rev. 1657, 1662–1663 (hereinafter Sack); *id.*, at 1663 ("Because these cases were considered noncriminal, police assigned domestic violence calls low priority and often did not respond to them for several hours or ignored them altogether"). In response to these realities, and emboldened by a well-known

1984 experiment by the Minneapolis police department,[Footnote 8] "many states enacted mandatory arrest statutes under which a police officer must arrest an abuser when the officer has probable cause to believe that a domestic assault has occurred or that a protection order has been violated." Developments in the Law: Legal Responses to Domestic Violence, 106 Harv. L. Rev. 1498, 1537 (1993). The purpose of these statutes was precisely to "counter police resistance to arrests in domestic violence cases by removing or restricting police officer discretion; mandatory arrest policies would increase police response and reduce batterer recidivism." Sack 1670.

Thus, when Colorado passed its statute in 1994, it joined the ranks of 15 States that mandated arrest for domestic violence offenses and 19 States that mandated arrest for domestic restraining order violations. See Developments in the Law, 106 Harv. L. Rev., at 1537, n. 68 (noting statutes in 1993); N. Miller, Institute for Law and Justice, A Law Enforcement and Prosecution Perspective 7, and n. 74, 8, and n. 90 (2003), http://www.ilj.org/dv/dvvawa2000.htm (as visited June 24, 2005, and available in Clerk of Court's case file) (listing Colorado among the many States that currently have mandatory arrest statutes).[Footnote 9]

Given the specific purpose of these statutes, there can be no doubt that the Colorado Legislature used the term "shall" advisedly in its domestic restraining order statute. While "shall" is probably best read to mean "may" in other Colorado statutes that seemingly mandate enforcement, cf. Colo. Rev. Stat. §31–4–112 (Lexis 2004) (police "*shall suppress* all riots, disturbances or breaches of the peace, *shall apprehend* all disorderly persons in the city ..." (emphases added)), it is clear that the elimination of police discretion was integral to Colorado and its fellow States' solution to the problem of underenforcement in domestic violence cases.[Footnote 10] Since the text of Colorado's statute perfectly captures this legislative purpose, it is hard to imagine what the Court has in mind when it insists on "some stronger indication from the Colorado Legislature." *Ante*, at 12.

While Colorado case law does not speak to the question, it is instructive that other state courts interpreting their analogous statutes have not only held that they eliminate the police's traditional discretion to refuse enforcement, but have also recognized that they create rights enforceable against the police under state law. For example, in *Nearing* v. *Weaver*, 295 Ore. 702, 670 P. 2d 137 (1983) (en banc), the court held that although the common law of negligence did not support a suit against the police for failing to enforce a domestic restraining order, the statute's mandatory directive formed the basis for the suit because it was "a specific duty imposed by statute for the benefit of individuals previously identified by judicial order." *Id.*, at 707, 670 P. 2d, at 140.[Footnote 11] In *Matthews* v. *Pickett County,* 996 S. W. 2d 162 (Tenn. 1999) (on certification to the Sixth Circuit), the court confirmed that the statute mandated arrest for violations of domestic restraining orders, and it held that the "public duty" defense to a negligence action was unavailable to the defendant police officers because the restraining order had created a "special duty" to protect the plaintiff. *Id.*, at 165. See also *Campbell* v. *Campbell*, 294 N. J. Super. 18, 24, 682 A. 2d 272, 274 (1996) (domestic restraining order statute "allows no discretion" with regard to arrest; "[t]he duty imposed on the police officer is ministerial"); *Donaldson* v. *Seattle*, 65 Wash. App. 661, 670, 831 P. 2d 1098, 1103 (1992) ("Generally, where an officer has legal grounds to make an arrest he has considerable discretion to do so. In regard to domestic violence, the rule is the reverse. If the officer has the legal grounds to arrest pursuant to the statute, he has a mandatory duty to make the arrest"). To what extent the Colorado Supreme Court would agree with the views of these courts is, of course, an open question, but it does seem rather brazen for the majority to assume that the Colorado Supreme Court would repudiate this consistent line of persuasive authority from other States.

Indeed, the Court fails to come to terms with the wave of domestic violence statutes that provides the crucial context for understanding Colorado's law. The Court concedes that, "in the specific context of domestic violence, mandatory-arrest statutes have been found in some States to be more mandatory than traditional mandatory-arrest statutes," *ante*, at 13, but that is a serious understatement. The difference is not a matter of degree, but of kind. Before this wave of statutes, the legal rule was one of discretion; as the Court shows, the "traditional," general mandatory arrest statutes have always been understood to be "mandatory" in name only, see *ante*, at 11. The innovation of the domestic violence statutes was to make police enforcement, not "more mandatory," but simply *mandatory*. If, as the Court says, the existence of a protected "entitlement" turns on whether "government officials may grant or deny it in their discretion," *ante*, at 7, the new mandatory statutes undeniably create an entitlement to police enforcement of restraining orders.

Perhaps recognizing this point, the Court glosses over the dispositive question—whether the police enjoyed discretion to deny enforcement—and focuses on a different question—which "precise means of enforcement," *ante*, at 14, were called for in this case. But that question is a red herring. The statute directs that, upon probable cause of a violation, "a peace officer shall arrest, or, if an arrest would be impractical under the circumstances, seek a warrant for the arrest of a restrained person." Colo. Rev. Stat. §18–6–803.5(3)(b) (Lexis 1999). Regardless of whether the enforcement called for in this case was arrest or the seeking of an arrest warrant (the answer to that question probably changed over the course of the night as the respondent gave the police more information about the husband's whereabouts), the crucial point is that, under the statute, the police were *required* to provide enforcement; *they lacked the discretion to do nothing*.[Footnote 12] The Court suggests that the fact that "enforcement" may encompass different acts infects any entitlement to enforcement with "indeterminacy." *Ante*, at 14. But this objection is also unfounded. Our cases have never required the object of an entitlement to be some mechanistic, unitary thing. Suppose a State entitled every citizen whose income was under a certain level to receive health care at a state clinic. The provision of health care is not a unitary thing— doctors and administrators must decide what tests are called for and what procedures are required, and these decisions often involve difficult applications of judgment. But it could not credibly be said that a citizen lacks an entitlement to health care simply because the content of that entitlement is not the same in every given situation. Similarly, the enforcement of a restraining order is not some amorphous, indeterminate thing. Under the statute, if the police have probable cause that a violation has occurred, enforcement consists of either making an immediate arrest or seeking a warrant and then executing an arrest— traditional, well-defined tasks that law enforcement officers perform every day.[Footnote 13]

The Court similarly errs in speculating that the Colorado Legislature may have mandated police enforcement of restraining orders for "various legitimate ends other than the conferral of a benefit on a specific class of people," *ante*, at 15; see also *ibid.* (noting that the "serving of public rather than private ends is the normal course of the criminal law"). While the Court's concern would have some bite were we faced with a broadly drawn statute directing, for example, that the police "*shall suppress* all riots," there is little doubt that the statute at issue in this case conferred a benefit "on a specific class of people"—namely, recipients of domestic restraining orders. Here, respondent applied for and was granted a restraining order from a Colorado trial judge, who found a risk of "irreparable injury" and found that "physical or emotional harm" would result if the husband were not excluded from the family home. 366 F. 3d, at 1143 (appendix to dissent of O'Brien, J.). As noted earlier, the restraining order required that the husband not "molest or disturb" the peace of respondent and the daughters, and it ordered (with limited exceptions) that the husband stay at least 100 yards away from the family home. *Ibid.*[Footnote 14] It also directed the police to "use every reasonable means to enforce this ... order," and to arrest or seek a warrant upon probable cause of a violation. *Id.*, at 1144. Under the terms of the statute, when the order issued, respondent and her daughters became " 'protected person[s].' " §18–6–803.5(1.5)(a) (" 'Protected person' means the person or persons identified in the restraining order as the person or persons for whose benefit the restraining order was issued").[Footnote 15] The statute criminalized the knowing violation of the restraining order, §18–6–803.5(1), and, as already discussed, the statute (as well as the order itself) mandated police enforcement, §§18–6–803.5(3)(a)–(b).[Footnote 16]

Because the statute's guarantee of police enforcement is triggered by, and operates only in reference to, a judge's granting of a restraining order in favor of an identified " 'protected person,' " there is simply no room to suggest that such a person has received merely an " 'incidental' " or " 'indirect' " benefit, see *ante*, at 18. As one state court put it, domestic restraining order statutes "identify with precision when, to whom, and under what circumstances police protection must be afforded. The legislative purpose in requiring the police to enforce individual restraining orders clearly is to protect the named persons for whose protection the order is issued, not to protect the community at large by general law enforcement activity." *Nearing*, 295 Ore., at 712, 670 P. 2d, at 143.[Footnote 17] Not only does the Court's doubt about whether Colorado's statute created an entitlement in a protected person fail to take seriously the purpose and nature of restraining orders, but it fails to account for the decisions by other state courts, see *supra* at 11–12, that recognize that such statutes and restraining orders create individual rights to police action.

IV

Given that Colorado law has quite clearly eliminated the police's discretion to deny enforcement, respondent is correct that she had much more than a "unilateral expectation" that the restraining order would be enforced; rather, she had a "legitimate claim of entitlement" to enforcement. *Roth,* 408 U. S., at 577. Recognizing respondent's property interest in the enforcement of her restraining order is fully consistent with our precedent. This Court has "made clear that the property interests protected by procedural due process extend well beyond actual ownership of real estate, chattels, or money." *Id.*, at 571–572. The "types of interests protected as 'property' are varied and, as often as not, intangible, 'relating to the whole domain of social and economic fact.' " *Logan* v. *Zimmerman Brush Co.*, 455 U. S. 422, 430 (1982); see also *Perry* v. *Sindermann*, 408 U. S. 593, 601 (1972) (" '[P]roperty' interests subject to procedural due process protection are not limited by a few rigid, technical forms. Rather, 'property' denotes a broad range of interests that are secured by 'existing rules or understandings' "). Thus, our cases have found "property" interests in a number of state-conferred benefits and services, including welfare benefits, *Goldberg* v. *Kelly*, 397 U. S. 254 (1970); disability benefits, *Mathews* v. *Eldridge*, 424 U. S. 319 (1976); public education, *Goss* v. *Lopez*, 419 U. S. 565 (1975); utility services, *Memphis Light, Gas & Water Div.* v. *Craft*, 436 U. S. 1 (1978); government employment, *Cleveland Bd. of Ed.* v. *Loudermill*, 470 U. S. 532 (1985); as well as in other entitlements that defy easy categorization, see, *e.g.*, *Bell* v.

Burson, 402 U. S. 535 (1971) (due process requires fair procedures before a driver's license may be revoked pending the adjudication of an accident claim); *Logan*, 455 U. S., at 431 (due process prohibits the arbitrary denial of a person's interest in adjudicating a claim before a state commission).

Police enforcement of a restraining order is a government service that is no less concrete and no less valuable than other government services, such as education.[Footnote 18] The relative novelty of recognizing this type of property interest is explained by the relative novelty of the domestic violence statutes creating a mandatory arrest duty; before this innovation, the unfettered discretion that characterized police enforcement defeated any citizen's "legitimate claim of entitlement" to this service. Novel or not, respondent's claim finds strong support in the principles that underlie our due process jurisprudence. In this case, Colorado law *guaranteed* the provision of a certain service, in certain defined circumstances, to a certain class of beneficiaries, and respondent reasonably relied on that guarantee. As we observed in *Roth*, "[i]t is a purpose of the ancient institution of property to protect those claims upon which people rely in their daily lives, reliance that must not be arbitrarily undermined." 408 U. S., at 577. Surely, if respondent had contracted with a private security firm to provide her and her daughters with protection from her husband, it would be apparent that she possessed a property interest in such a contract. Here, Colorado undertook a comparable obligation, and respondent— with restraining order in hand—justifiably relied on that undertaking. Respondent's claim of entitlement to this promised service is no less legitimate than the other claims our cases have upheld, and no less concrete than a hypothetical agreement with a private firm.[Footnote 19] The fact that it is based on a statutory enactment and a judicial order entered for her special protection, rather than on a formal contract, does not provide a principled basis for refusing to consider it "property" worthy of constitutional protection.[Footnote 20]

V

Because respondent had a property interest in the enforcement of the restraining order, state officials could not deprive her of that interest without observing fair procedures.[Footnote 21] Her description of the police behavior in this case and the department's callous policy of failing to respond properly to reports of restraining order violations clearly alleges a due process violation. At the very least, due process requires that the relevant state decisionmaker *listen* to the claimant and then *apply the relevant criteria* in reaching his decision.[Footnote 22] The failure to observe these minimal procedural safeguards creates an unacceptable risk of arbitrary and "erroneous deprivation[s]," *Mathews*, 424 U. S., at 335. According to respondent's complaint—which we must construe liberally at this early stage in the litigation, see *Swierkiewicz* v. *Sorema N. A.,* 534 U. S. 506, 514 (2002)—the process she was afforded by the police constituted nothing more than a " 'sham or a pretense.' " *Joint Anti&nbhyph;Fascist Refugee Comm.* v. *McGrath,* 341 U. S. 123, 164 (1951) (Frankfurter, J., concurring).

Accordingly, I respectfully dissent.[17]

---

[17] Stevens, John P. "Castle Rock v. Gonzales, 545 U.S. 748 (2005)." *Justia Law*, US Supreme Court, 5 June 2005, supreme.justia.com/cases/federal/us/545/748/.

We must continue fighting the grossly unfair treatment of vulnerable victims of domestic violence. America's problem with violence and the men who perpetrate it and those who protect the abusers will continue if nobody objects.

Is the current treatment of women and children alright with you? Have you ever been so frightened that you needed to call the police? If not, consider yourself lucky. The odds that if you have not needed the police to come to your aid, you will. At some point, you will. Do you want today's police force ignoring you or your child's call for help?

Perhaps it is your sister, your best friend, your neighbor who needs help from an abusive partner. Maybe it will be your son, his best friend, or a cousin. Chances are you are directly related to a victim of domestic violence. And chances are you do not know it, not for sure.

Maybe your friend tells you about how angry her husband gets. Perhaps she likes dropping by unexpected yet arrives frazzled. She is probably escaping her abuser's latest explosion of anger and vulgarity.

Or maybe your girlfriend makes one too many excuses for why she can't meet you in public. She may be controlled, or she may be bruised and bandaged, healing from the latest beating her partner delivered last night.

If you are an educator, you know the look of the distressed child who is struggling at home. If you have had a chance to make any connections, words will come out that let you know he is a victim as well as the mother.

Every day across millions of America women and their children are victims of domestic violence. The women are trapped and oppressed in their homes in 2020. American must change the way it responds and deals with domestic violence. No longer with the crumbs off the table of the US Justice Department suffice.

American Women remember the fight women fought to gain the right to vote. Use our political power and majority in American society to demand change. Use this historic anniversary of most American women gaining the right to vote. Let us bring all our sisters along to a better place where women's rights are honored every day. Where women and children are free from violence in their daily lives. And when violence is perpetrated upon women and children, the US Justice system will apply US law and hold the guilty accountable.

One of the first changes that should be made is to see American police departments across the nation add women to their force until they reach 50.8%. Bring women into the police force could only bring about changes for the better for every community. Imagine what the response would be for the victim, as well as the abuser if a woman with a badge and gun should up to investigate the domestic disturbance. We can no longer accept the abuse of power and brutality that comes from a male-dominated police force.

Truth-in-Spending

Due to the incredible advances seen in the high-tech industry, we move through our daily lives with information and data pouring out of our devices and screens. With all the hardware and software now in place in our everyday lives, why would we accept the standards of yesteryear? Why are we still accepting the painfully slow and inefficiency of government workers? They are not asked to go work in the hot sun or with lunch breaks or a restroom break. Most sit at a desk with a computer, phone, and air-conditioning. They are free to get up and use the restroom or go to lunch within their scheduled time.

Yet with all this freedom and financial security government jobs provide, American citizens are continually subjected to poor or indifferent customer service. Why shouldn't we expect a certain level of humanity and respect from our government workers? It is not as though we are training a pet to speak. We are asking humans, American humans who are given a fair salary and a buffet of benefits to bring their best game face to work. They just need to be nice and smile on the days they want to be paid, otherwise, they can be free to a frowny sourpuss to their family and friends. Spare us taxpayers, we are providing your check. Remember that.

Once basic manners are addressed, why can't we have online access to the operating numbers? I would like to see how many people are being helped today at the DA's battered woman's program. Were they given a protection order, offered additional services, or were they just made to show up and nothing happened? The victim was sent home with nothing to show for her time or any help or hope for protection from her abuser.

I would like to see government workers have their clock in time appear when they arrive, leave for lunch, and what time they clock out. I want to be able to log on to a department and see how many government workers are getting paid that minute as well as how many citizens are being helped.

That can all be done with the software available and existing hardware. The will simply has to be there. The government is not going to ask itself to be accountable and transparent. That would be our job, citizens of the United States. Taxpayers who make vote for presidents and policies.

An approach to accountability and transparency can be taken from the Truth-in-Lending (TILA) Act. In order to protect consumers against inaccurate and unfair billing and credit practices, the TILA requires lenders to provide loan cost information so that consumers can comparison shop for certain types of loans. A Truth-in-Lending Disclosure Statement provides information about the costs of your credit. You receive a Truth-in-Lending disclosure twice: an initial disclosure when you apply for a mortgage loan, and a final disclosure before closing.[18]

If we apply this concept to our inefficient government departments, bureaus, divisions, agencies, etc. we should get a Truth-in-Spending disclosure explaining what they plan to do with money. Each year taxpayers should also receive a concluding disclosure that showed exactly how much was spent, in what areas, and how many citizens were helped.

Use an American Pie graph, citizens would be able to clearly see how much the department or agency received, how many staff members were paid, and with what was left, how many American citizens were helped. If those pie slices are not acceptable, we can pressure the departments to run more efficiently.

---

[18] "What Is a Truth-in-Lending Disclosure for a Mortgage Loan?" Consumer Financial Protection Bureau, 13 Sept. 2017, www.consumerfinance.gov/ask-cfpb/what-is-a-truth-in-lending-disclosure-en-180/.

Right now, Americans do not expect any accountability or transparency by government agencies. Let us change that by demanding the US government provide regular information on their civil servant performance and expenditures.

If we fly to the moon, transfer the power of government smoothly every four years, track the national debt by the dollar and by the second, win wars around the world, we can certainly handle some transparency and accountability.

We, the American people, are the 'owners' of this business we call, American Democracy. It is up to us to demand better performance from our government workers.

FINAL THOUGHTS

I have made the arduous trek up the treacherous US justice system mountain in search of protection, freedom, justice, and peace. As a survivor of brutal and unrelenting domestic violence, I wrote this book as a testament to my survival so that others will know the journey is possible.

My writing is also my effort to bring an awareness that justice in America for women and children has eroded faster than our foremothers would have ever imagined. We cannot allow their hard work to slip through our complacent hands. We must knock down the false fronts that the US government has presented to women and the world.

As I approach my 60th year walking this planet, I cannot help but think about the fact I have spent nearly a third of my life dealing with this individual. Half of that time I was running from him. Running for my life and the life of my children. Running in search of peace and happiness.

These are supposed to be fundamental rights protected for me as an American. Yet, as a woman in American in 2020, my experience has been anything but just. I have seen our family abuser accommodated and promoted in the legal system. All the while services, protection, and justice have been denied to me and my children.

I survived years of unrelenting domestic violence in every shade it comes in: physical, emotional, sexual, psychological, financial, and legal. abuse. The small victories I gained along the way provided the confidence I desperately needed to continue, pushing my exhausted and battered soul to continue fighting for justice.

Along my journey for justice, I encountered many who were able to help but did not. Individuals who had the choice to help or hinder a mother, a victim of unrelenting domestic violence, and chose the latter. I did not expect an outpouring of warmth and compassion, but what I did not expect from my government agencies was the consistent cold, outright rejection. Protection designed by the Justice Department to protect women and children like us was denied by women.

My mind spins trying to understand how we have come from 100 years of winning the right to be recognized by the US government to being dismissed by liberated women. with all their rights bestowed upon, actively working to deny me justice.

We have been wronged for so long, I do not want to see an overhaul or reform. Women and children must have their own department to meet the complex needs of giving birth and raising children. American children deserve a voice. Not just when they turn 18 years old. That is a voting requirement. Why can't children voice their opinions? On their living situation at home and conditions at school.

Their voices should be given a place to be heard. From their better policies can be created with real input from those who must live with it, at home and at school. Are we not trying to create the best society? How can we ignore the future generation, and only acknowledge them the moment they turn 18 years old?

American children could be experiencing hands-on democracy. They would view their world and offer solutions that we adults just do not see. By allowing children to have a say in the government, they will become more interested in our government system. If we do our job right, we will raise them to honor, uphold, and continually improve the American system.

We must do a better job of protecting our most vulnerable citizens. It is critical that we protect American children and their mothers from violence, because they are unquestionably essential to our future.

Made in United States
Troutdale, OR
05/26/2024

20142160R00099